Also-Space, From Hot to Something Else:

How Indonesian Art Initiatives Have Reinvented Networking

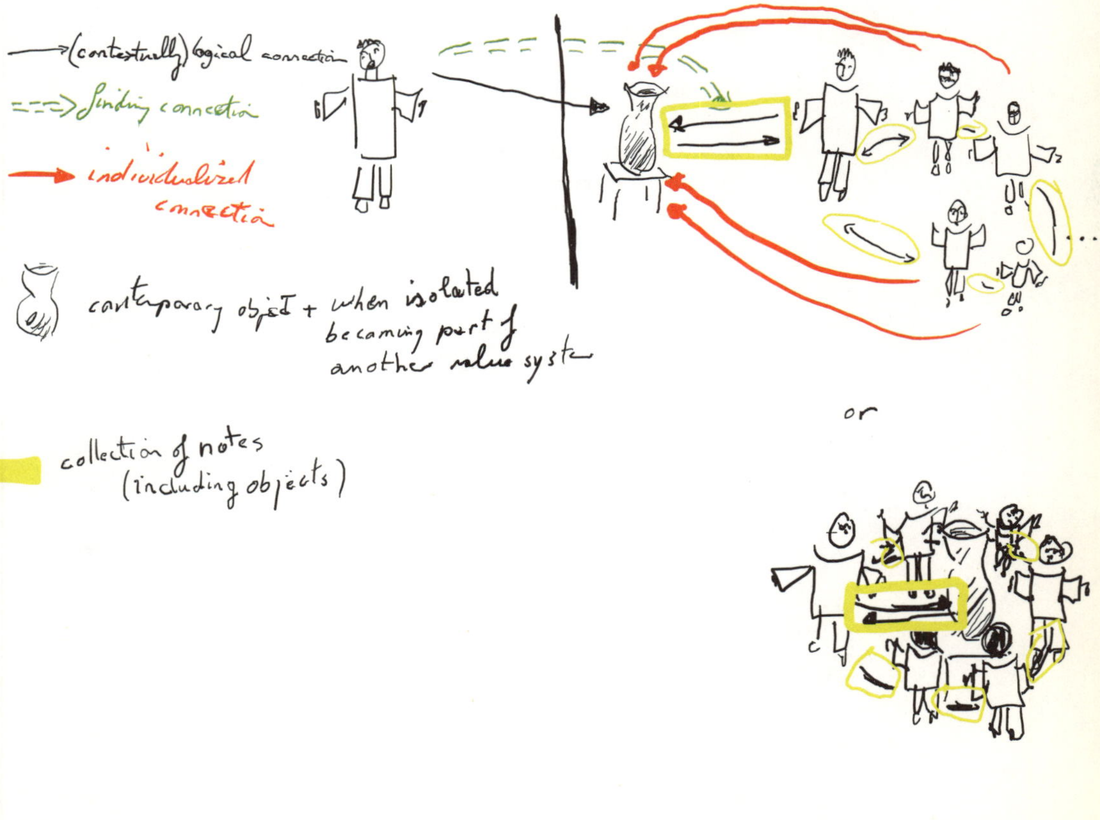

reinaart vanhoe

table of contents

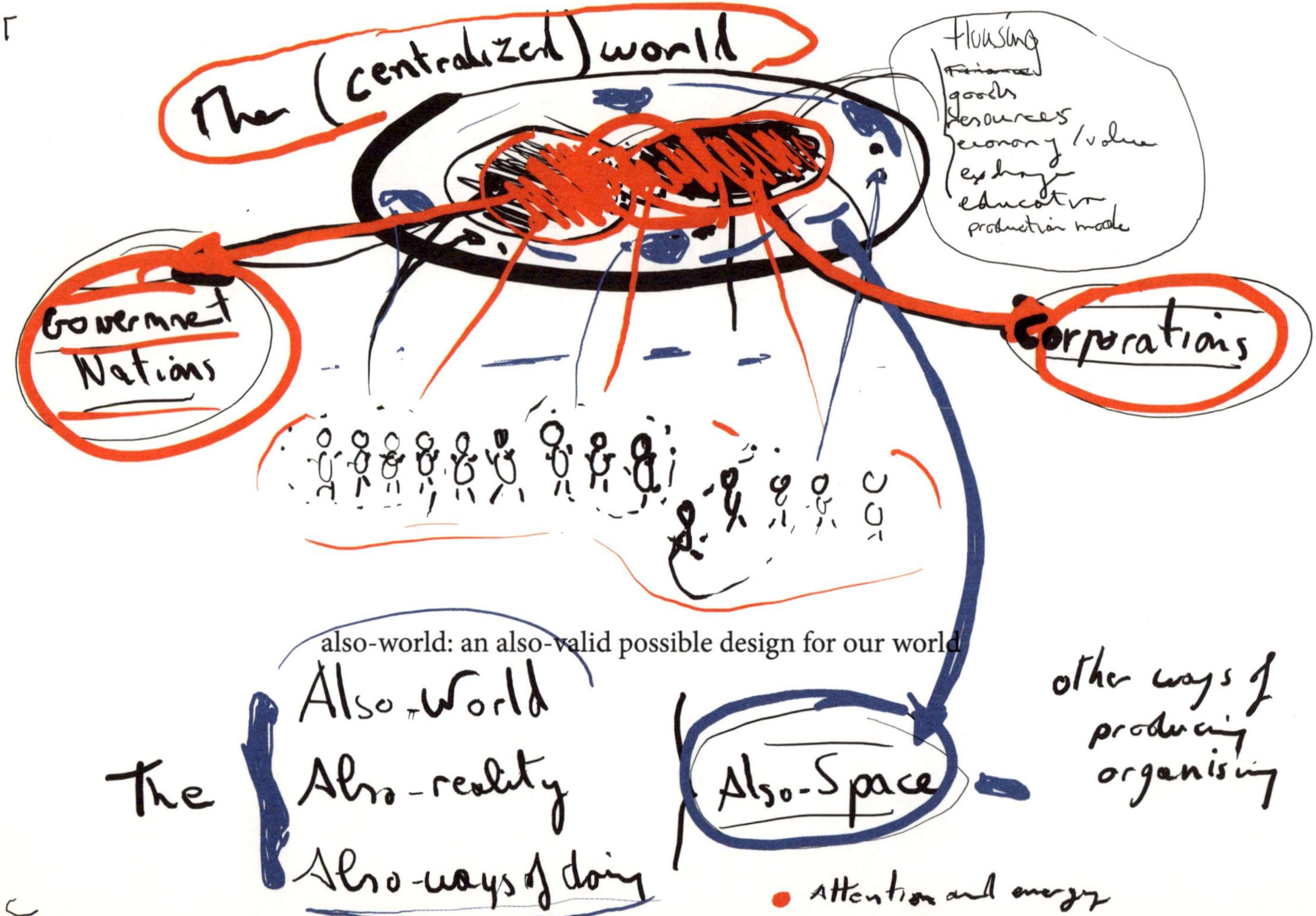

also-world: an also-valid possible design for our world

Foreword

Although contemporary art in Indonesia is completely integrated within the global art discourse, the fundamental context of Indonesian artists is in fact quite different from that of the contemporary Western artistic practice, in which notions of individuality and 'autonomy' play a key role. This perspective, at least in its current manifestation, is based on a neo-liberal worldview focused more or less entirely on the pursuit of individual success. However, what is often missing from this perspective is an awareness of local networks, and a contextual (as opposed to purely conceptual) way of thinking and acting.

Indonesian artists' initiatives, on the other hand, tend to think and work from the perspective of the communities of which they are already a part. This is quite different from the Western notion of 'community art', as it addresses fundamentally different approaches to community and networking. Indonesian artists work from an understanding that they are organically and inevitably connected to various networks, whereas Western artists tend to proactively seek out and connect to networks from an individualist position.

This book focuses mainly on the Jakarta-based artists' initiative ruangrupa, and to a lesser degree on a number of other Indonesian artists and initiatives (Homeshop, Jatiwangi Art Factory, Lifepatch, Moelyono, Wok the Rock), as case studies of how Indonesian artists organise and manifest themselves individually as well as collectively.

Recurring themes also include the author's ongoing efforts in formulating proposals of a '(g)Locally Embedded Art Practice' ('gLEAP') and of the 'also-space' as approaches to re-evaluating the production and positioning of artists. How can we develop an artistic practice that does not define itself as 'alternative' or 'in opposition' to the society in which it exists, but rather as an integral part of the various communities in which the artist functions, produces and lives, and is thus very much a part of?

Chapter 1 provides a theoretical as well as practical overview of the current cultural and social constellation in which the author appears to find himself.

Chapter 2 is a detailed investigation of the Jakarta-based artists' collective ruangrupa: how it functions, how it has evolved throughout the years, and how it may serve as an example for a 'gLEAP' practice.

Chapter 3 investigates the idea of 'also-space' as a model for reformulating one's artistic practice; this chapter also examines a few other Indonesian artists and artists' initiatives as examples of how artists may integrate more organically their working practice with their everyday activities.

This research was conducted and written by reinaart vanhoe at the Research Centre Creating 010, Rotterdam University of Applied Sciences, and the Willem de Kooning Academy, Rotterdam University of Applied Sciences. Part of the field research was conducted during a residency by the author at KUNCI Cultural Studies Center, Yogyakarta, Indonesia, in 2014.

Editor's note: Many of the texts quoted in this publication were written directly in English, by international artists and researchers who may not necessarily be fluent in this language, but for whom English is simply the necessary medium for communicating with a global contemporary audience. Out of respect for all the individuals quoted, we have left their texts exactly as they were. We sincerely believe that any possible idiosyncrasies in their use of the English language do not in any way diminish the substance or eloquence of their words.

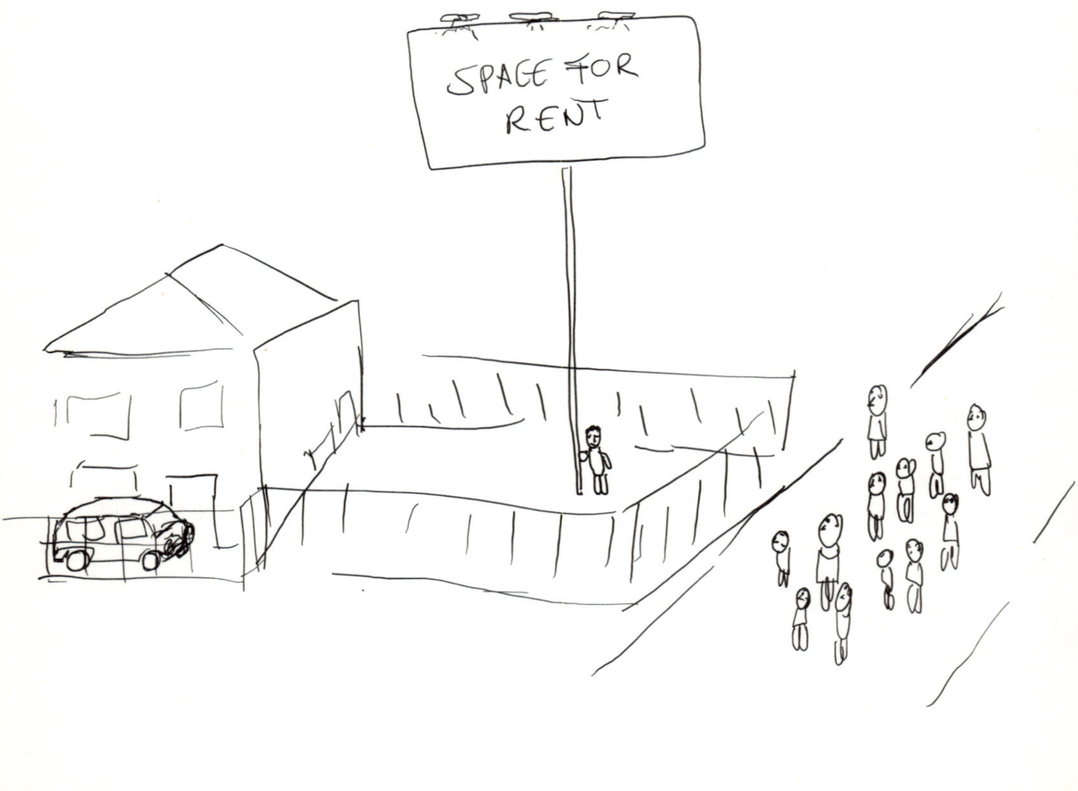

Chapter 1:

From Europe to elsewhere

1.1 Introduction

The starting point for this publication is my ongoing sense of doubt regarding my own artistic practice and how this practice, however authentic and independent-minded it may be, is in fact completely integrated within a world focused on achieving an individual and successful art career, and everything else that is constructed around that endeavour. It is a world which I and many others rebel against, but which we are also entirely a part of, in all of our activities and the systems in which we operate. This system has been variously called 'liberal individualism', 'neoliberalism', etc. As a young artist, I imagined that alternative art spaces could help define an artistic practice that would show me a way out of this dilemma.

I was born and raised in Belgium and moved to the Netherlands around 1995, hoping to benefit from the abundance of alternative art spaces[1] being set up here in those days.[2] Today, alternative (art) spaces can be defined as spaces ranging from artist-run initiatives to institutionalised art centres that grew out of the alternative culture and counterculture, such as 'De Appel' in Amsterdam. But in fact the alternative space has often been little more than a myth. Nowadays artists who operate in the margins of contemporary art are also involved in, and are a part of, the mainstream culture; a culture that is dominated by neo-liberal values, a world that artists often resist in their artistic practice. Alternative (art) spaces could be defined here as spaces where artists can test their ideas, show their work, develop their vocabulary, and be in dialogue with an audience that mainly consists of colleague artists, the artists' inner circle, and art-related professionals. Although being an open place for production and discourse, the alternative space, unlike the 'also-space' (which I shall explain later in this book) begins from the perspective that the artist, and the artist alone, is at the centre of the work.

These days however, the traditional division between 'alternative' and 'mainstream' institutions no longer works. Chantal Mouffe explains that artistic and cultural production (also of the alternative and/or critical variety) plays an important role in the process of capital valorisation:

> *'Can artistic practices still play a critical role in a society where the differences between art and advertizing have become blurred and where artists and cultural workers have become a necessary part of capitalist production? Scrutinizing the "new spirit of capitalism" Luc Boltanski and Eve Chiapello[3] have shown how the demands for autonomy of the new movements of the 1960's had been harnessed in the development of the post-Fordist networked economy and transformed in new forms of control. The aesthetic strategies of the counter-culture: the search for authenticity, the ideal of self-management, the anti-hierarchical exigency, are now used in order to promote the conditions required by the current mode of capitalist regulation, replacing the disciplinary framework characteristic of the Fordist period. Nowadays artistic and cultural production*

---

1 Terms such as 'alternative art', 'critical art', 'alternative art institutions' or even 'art spaces' can be ambiguous, all depending on what kind of art and artists they happen to be referring to.

2 For example, De Fabriek and MUU in Eindhoven; Lokaal 01 in Breda and Antwerp, Ruimte X, De Verschijning and Van de nieuwe dingen in Tilburg; De Melkfabriek and Artis in Den Bosch; Extrapool and Paraplufabriek in Nijmegen; Stichting Filmstad in The Hague; Fotomania and Vaalserberg in Rotterdam; W139 and P//////AKT in Amsterdam; the AVE festival in Arnhem; the Impakt festival in Utrecht; etc.

3 Luc Boltanski and Eve Chiapello, *The New Spirit of Capitalism*, London, Verso, 2005.

play a central role in the process of capital valorization and, through "neo-management", artistic critique has become an important element of capitalist productivity.'

Chantal Mouffe, 'Artistic Activism and Agonistic Spaces', in: ART&RESEARCH: A Journal of Ideas, Contexts and Methods, Vol. 1, No. 2, Summer 2007.

Being aware of this condition, artists could begin to reconsider their position within society, rather than seeing themselves as 'alternative', as pseudo-semi-outsiders. Perhaps then we might gain some insight into what artists could or should be doing after the successive waves of avant-garde, conceptualism, institutional critique, relational aesthetics, etc. This is why I have titled this publication 'Also-Space, From Hot to Something Else': it suggests that we are heading somewhere, only we don't know where yet. What comes next, after being modern, hip and fashionable?

What Chantal Mouffe describes in the quotation above is a global phenomenon. How does this apply to the situation of artists in the Netherlands today?

In the Netherlands, the identity and position of artists in society is subject of intense and passionate debate, as well as cynical indifference, for a variety of reasons. As artists in their artistic practice seem increasingly stuck in a critique of a capitalist-liberal lifestyle of which they themselves are a part, just like everybody else, society at large seems to consider artists as representatives of a cultural elite that apparently gather in obscure spaces, cut off from the common people.[4] At the same time, the romantic cliché of the artist is being co-opted as never before in advertising campaigns promoting real estate projects, city trips and a variety of other merchandise and services, as part of a pre-packaged lifestyle with all the appropriate paraphernalia.[5] Everybody expects the artist to produce something of value to them: social housing corporations, government agencies, collectors, citizens and private enterprises all want to work together with artists because they expect artists to be able to cast a different light on a variety of socially relevant issues.

Some art platforms often also focus on public spaces or on the social environment and social cohesion, such as Jeanne van Heeswijk's Freehouse (Rotterdam), NAC (also Rotterdam) and Stroom (The Hague). Still, there seems to be huge discrepancy between the priorities of artists and the expectations of other parties as to what art exactly can deliver. Artists too often still work from a perspective of specialists, while other parties tend to think from an expectation that art should contribute something positive or beneficial. Though both positions are probably to be expected, it might be interesting for a change to challenge this status quo. As the Rotterdam cultural philosopher Henk Oosterling stated in an interview with the magazine *rekto:verso*:

'Indeed, we should be drawing our conclusions from the fact that art is now everywhere. That our age-old avant-garde position is now entirely behind us, because everyone is now avant-garde. Only when you realise as an artist that such an autonomous position no longer exists, can you start working from a new position. This means that artists should get over their fear of making compromises, of becoming aesthetically and artistically corrupted. This is the big "problem" of the "network thinking" which I encourage: you're always collaborating in this system. There is no "outside" because everything is connected to everything else. Only when you realise this can you get to work and celebrate your creativity.' [6]

---

4 Joost de Vries, in an interview with Bas Heijne, 'Het gaat niet om kunst, het is een sociale strijd' ('It's not about art, it's a social struggle'), in: *De Groene Amsterdammer*, February 23, 2011.

5 See Richard Florida, *The Rise of the Creative Class*, 2002.

6 Wouter Hillaert and Tom Viaene, 'De kunstenaar als publieke werker. Een gesprek met Henk Oosterling', in: *rekto:verso*, no. 54, November-December 2012.

In other words, artists need to become more aware of, and learn to relate to, the various networks in which they already find themselves. For Oosterling, an artist should learn to function rather as a networker. This is indeed important, but it is only one step, one aspect. The stereotype of the modern or contemporary artist, the individual author, remains intact, even though we know that it is a myth.[7] This paradigm which many of us (including Oosterling) persist in defending needs to be seriously reconsidered, as does the very concept of the avant-garde. In many socially engaged or critical projects, the artworks themselves often may be *conceptually* sound, but *contextually* there is little connection with what is actually going on at the local level. There is simply too little interest in actually making connections in the real world. The work is understood within artistic circles as socially critical and engaged art, however outside these circles this engagement often means very little in practice.

I do not pretend in this book to propose a practical solution to this situation, or even a keen analysis that might serve as a call to arms. However, through my long personal involvement with the Indonesian artists' initiative ruangrupa, as well as my experiences as an artist and educator, I have developed a number of insights which I believe may be of some use in reformulating and re-evaluating what it means to be an artist. This begins by rediscovering or reformulating the relationship between our daily activities and our artistic/professional production. Can we learn from artistic and living practices that are based, whether consciously or not, on the idea of *acting contextually*? Practices, such as ruangrupa, that consciously relate and connect their own activities to the context and living environment in which the work is produced?

As the capitalist model becomes increasingly dominant, resulting in a gradual erosion of the welfare state, people are busy reorganising a number of social, organisational and production models, in order to regain control of, and give shape to, their daily life, preoccupations and production. Contemporary artists have been working on such themes for some time now; consider for example the emergence of relational aesthetics, community art, participatory art and institutional critique in 1990s. Everything I have said about the limitations of alternative spaces also applies to these practices. This is why I wish to introduce here a concept which I have called gLEAP, or (g)Locally Embedded Art Practice, which I will explain in more detail in chapter 3 of this publication. For now, suffice to say that this concept of gLEAP has little or nothing in common with relational aesthetics and other similar alternative art movements.

Rather, gLEAP focuses on the environment itself, the context, unlike relational aesthetics where the context somehow always ends up being the artists and their audience.[8] Nor should gLEAP be considered as some form of community art or participatory art. Rather, the point I am making here is that artists should not only understand their context, but also work with this context in what I call a *contextually logical* way, alone or with others (and in a way that is always open to others, in whatever role may be appropriate in each particular context).

In this research I will be examining a specific practical case in order to demonstrate the significance of a 'locally embedded' art practice; a practice based on exchange, shared ownership, informal collaborations and long-term relationships. How does an artist or a collective set up such an artistic practice? What is the nature and form of their production, both artistic and otherwise? Where and when does the 'public moment' take place? Which methodologies are most suitable to such a practice? What are the distinguishing characteristics of its aesthetics? Etc.

Since I am also writing this research from my own professional perspective as an art educator, and that this publication is being realised in collaboration with Creating 010, a Research Centre of the Rotterdam University of Applied Sciences, of which the Willem de Kooning

[7] See for instance Michel Foucault, *What is an Author.*

[8] Claire Bishop, 'Antagonism and Relational Aesthetics', in: *October* (magazine), No. 110, Fall 2004, pp. 51-79.

Academy (the art and design school where I teach) is also a part, I feel compelled to address the role that art education could or should play in the type of practice I am proposing here. I believe that we should start by realising quite simply that when citizens start fundamentally redesigning their living environment, as it is now happening all around the world, this poses a huge challenge as well as an opportunity for the arts.

A few examples:
– Citizens initiate projects and organise themselves: for example, Leeszaal Rotterdam West (a grassroots library in Rotterdam), We Are Here (a collective of refugees in the Netherlands), SolidarityNYC (a solidarity economy collective in New York City); and various movements such as guerrilla gardening, freeganism, etc.
– New kinds of institutions are being set up: Rotterdam Vakmanstad Skillcity (an institute for social-educational career guidance), Jeanne van Heeswijk's Freehouse (which makes physical, social and organisational space available for local initiatives and projects), Institute for Human Activities (an artistic research project focusing on economic inequality), food banks in all major cities, etc.
– An increasing number of proposals for new models of society and production: peer-to-peer economy, 'pirate' parties in legislatures throughout Europe, critical art institutes such as Casco (Utrecht), 16 Beaver Group (New York City) and Constant (Brussels); critical TV news programmes such as Tegenlicht/Mensen van nu, broadcast by the VPRO in the Netherlands; critical information technology institutes such as Bricolabs; the Raspberry Pi community, etc.
– The concept of intellectual property ('copyright', 'originality', etc.) is increasingly being questioned through new models focusing instead on sharing (GNU General Public License, Creative Commons licenses, 'social design', online platforms such as Nettime and the Institute of Network Cultures (both founded by the Dutch media theorist and critic Geert Lovink).
– New insights in labour, production and value: renewed focus on the commons, for example through time banking or time-based currency; online platforms for human-oriented economic development such as Commons Transition, GNUnion and the Basic Income Earth Network; local barter currencies such as De Zuiderling (South Rotterdam), social research institutes such as Mies (the Netherlands), etc.

The very fact that there is a term to describe something, usually means that individuals and groups have already been dealing with these issues for some time. And yet, a change of mentality is not something that happens overnight. How should we take the next step, who will be taking these steps, and how should an artist act within the perspective of a changing world? One thing is for certain, the 'art world' that we teach our students about in art academies is in a very difficult predicament. On one hand, official art education in the Netherlands is still expected to adhere to government policy, which is focused on the priorities of a neo-liberal market economy. At the same time, the romanticist expectations of art are still very much present, as can be seen for example in the practice of 'Dutch artist and innovator' [9] Daan Roosegaarde. This means that concepts such as creativity, pioneering, participation and cultural entrepreneurship are only understood in the context of individual endeavour, competitiveness, the restriction of knowledge, profit maximisation, privatisation, etc. This has also been described by critical theorists such as Gerald Raunig and Pascal Gielen; the cover text of Gielen's book 'The Murmuring of the Artistic Multitude' indeed states that:

> *'[...] the globalized art scene is an ideal production entity for economic exploitation. These days the work ethic of the art world with its ever-present young dynamic, flexible*

[9] From the artist's website: *https://www.studioroosegaarde.net/info/about-daan/*

working hours, thematic approach, short-term contracts or lack of contracts and its unlimited, energetic freedom is capitalized within the cultural industry and has been converted into a standard production model. In the glow of the creative cities and the creative industry governments embrace this post-Henry Ford work model and seamlessly link it to the globally dominant neo liberal market economy.' [10]

In other words, a society focused on individual performance and individual responsibility. This is also the perspective according to which art academies are evaluated. One of the goals of this research is to help shed some light on this discrepancy between the social role students are in fact being prepared for (cultural entrepreneurs) and how they are being told to think of themselves (critical, engaged thinkers), and also to propose a possible way forward: by encouraging artists to design, experiment, think and act from an authentically social perspective. New designs for social living, or in other words: from hot to something else.

1.2 'From Hot to Something Else'

'From Hot to Something Else' is an artwork by Pierre Bismuth in De Singel in Antwerp, Belgium (see side text). The artwork, realised in 2006, consists of seven words spray-painted on the walls at different locations throughout the complex. The first word, 'Hot', is written on the wall of an office space; another word can be found near the cloakroom; yet another can be seen from the main road, etc. Though the actual location of the words throughout the complex does not seem to follow any particular order or system, an attentive observer can deduce that the first word is 'Hot' and that each word is a synonym of the previous and following words: From 'Hot' to 'Spicy' to 'Piquant', 'Sparkling', 'Glimmering', 'Dazzling', and finally 'Radiant'.

One of the things I really like about this artwork is that there are a number of ways of encountering it; it is an active artwork that communicates differently to different viewers in different situations, who may happen to approach the artwork passively or actively. The work is implemented within the building and relates to the building's function in what I call a contextually logical way. By presenting this artwork, De Singel seems to be asking itself: where are we going, what will our future world look like, which aesthetics will apply in such a world? Personally I see 'From Hot to Something Else' as a critique of how our everyday environments are constructed. We want everything to look smooth and polished, stylish and 'hot', so that we can go on telling ourselves that everything is fine. But everything is not fine, which is why we really need to start looking for something else. We're still not quite sure yet what that 'Something Else' will be, but we can definitely sense that we have started moving.

Obviously this is my own interpretation of this artwork, which also triggers a number of my own recurring concerns; when artistic practices (which may in and of themselves be quite interesting) go no further than a mere representation of social processes, and when artists practice the very same methods as an aggressively capitalist, hegemony-oriented art market, how can that 'Something

De Singel is a large and multidisciplinary 'international arts campus' in Antwerp, Belgium.

The main building provides a platform for the production and presentation of mostly performative arts such as theatre, music and dance, but there is also an active programme for visual art and architecture. The campus also accommodates a number of cultural and educational organisations such as the Antwerp Conservatory, a radio station, a library, offices, lecture halls, a grand café, etc. De Singel was based upon the vision of the Flemish composer Peter Benoit in the late 19th century. Benoit's ideas about art education went further than merely training artists and musicians; his dream was to engage the population of the city in the international world of music and theatre, by linking the conservatory to a concert venue where music students and the general public would come together in their appreciation of fine music.

. . .

[10] Source: *http://www.valiz.nl/en/TheMurmuringoftheArtisticMultitude*

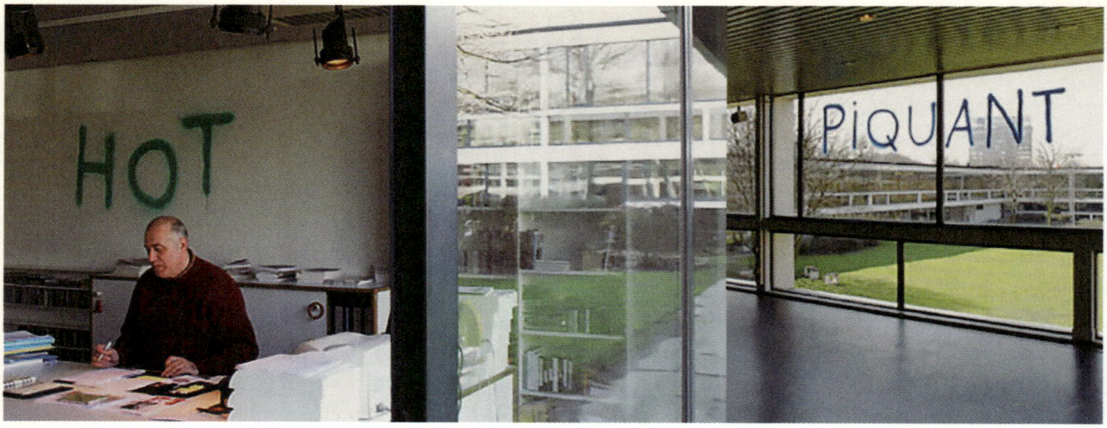

Else' ever come into being? What would be the working methods of such a 'Something Else'? What would be the aesthetics resulting from these methods?

What do I recognise in this artwork by Pierre Bismuth:
– The artwork is in a sense part of the building, rather than an 'object' being 'exhibited'. The public consists of people who happen to be passing by as they conduct their unrelated business (though usually of a cultural nature) in the complex, rather than typical gallery/museum viewers.
– The artwork questions our artistic/cultural production, and the place and function of this production in public spaces.
– Bismuth's artwork relates in a contextually logical way to its environment. This is also how I like to develop my own work, according to a system which I call PPL: place, position, and logic of context. What is the place; for whom, what or where am I making this artwork? How do I position myself in this situation? And what is the logic of how I relate to this context, to this place and position?
– The public is merely provided with an opportunity to encounter the artwork. On one hand, the artwork's raw aesthetic makes it hard to ignore, yet there is a degree of ambiguity in its role and position within its environment: at first glance it may seem like a piece of unauthorised graffiti.
– The artwork exists in an environment surrounded by other (professional) activities.

On the other hand:
– The artwork is still located in a building whose function is artistic production and presentation. This public space is in fact no more than semi-public, artificially separated from its environment, a place for a specific category of professions or specialisms. (What kind of people find themselves in this building, as opposed to what happens outside the building?)
– Though this particular artwork definitely appeals to

The older generation of living artists have experienced firsthand the evolution of modern and contemporary visual art. They have witnessed its development from a Western-oriented practice to a global platform of artistic exchange. They have seen it crystallise into an interestingly perverse domain of visual production. This includes an extensive production of sincerely engaged artistic practices. Alternative art and critical practices have gradually become institutionalised and of course represent substantial commercial value. There are many artists, many valued colleagues, many initiatives and festivals, many new collectors, a new young public, etc. A quick glance through the e-flux newsletter is enough to become convinced of the broad acceptance of an engaged, critical, rebellious artistic practice. And yet, there is a profound discomfort within the alternative arts, whether it takes place in commercial or non-commercial spaces. The German artist Hito Steyerl described this discomfort as follows:

'How do we make art and to whom do we address it amidst the over-production of idea's and goods the world produces. A destructive world, illustrated by the artworks of our so-called critical art-practice. We need to reconsider our art-practice, we need to reconsider the places

me, I still find myself wondering whether its materialisation has really been thought through as much as it could be.
– The practice of an artist mostly takes place within the vocabulary and discourse of the art world. Although an artwork, or an artist's body of work, may refer extensively to public spaces, it often doesn't really engage with these spaces themselves, but instead connects to a dialogue within an art scene, a world of galleries, museums and other art institutions.

An alternative model has been proposed by P. Gielen, C. van Winkel and K. Zwaan: the concept of the multitasking 'hybrid artist' [11] active in a variety of creative disciplines. However this definition remains limited to the professional field of art and design. I believe we must look one step further. In the practice of art and design, we must be willing to assume different roles and positions in the development and sharing of knowledge within our own social and cultural environments. Sometimes I will be a volunteer, sometimes a participant, an assistant, a maker, a member of the public, a technician, a neighbour, an artist, etc., without any of this being seen as an 'unusual' or even 'alternative' practice. In this sense, an artist is always a hybrid artist.

1.3 Practical examples, an introduction

Ruangrupa and HomeShop, two artists' initiatives, one in Jakarta, the other in Beijing.

I will be mainly using the example of ruangrupa, an artists' initiative from Jakarta, Indonesia, in order to address a number of points related to my concept of (g)Locally Embedded Art Practice (gLEAP, which have briefly I touched upon earlier in this chapter will describe in detail in chapter 3), and to illustrate this concept more concretely for young Western artists. I also see this research as an opportunity to provide feedback to a new generation of ruangrupa members.

My original intention for this research was to present a comparison between ruangrupa and an artists' initiative from Beijing called HomeShop.[12] Both ruangrupa and HomeShop are excellent examples in my opinion of initiatives that relate to their environment in a contextually logical way, with a generous open-door policy that encourages people to come in, sit around the table, work on plans or simply start a conversation.

where it takes place. We need to reconsider our materialization.'

Hito Steyerl, 'Politics of Art', in: e-flux journal, No. 21, December 2010.

. . .

See also the introduction to a presentation by Renzo Martens at V2_, Institute for the Unstable Media, an interdisciplinary centre for art and media technology in Rotterdam:

'On March 6, artist Renzo Martens provided an in-depth look at the workflow behind the chocolate sculptures that are sold through the Institute for Human Activities pop-up store at V2_. The IHA asserts that even when art critically engages with global inequalities, it most often solely brings beauty, jobs, and opportunity to the places where such art is exhibited, discussed and sold – like London, New York and Berlin and not where it has been produced.'

Source: *http://v2.nl/events/lectureby-renzo-martens*

. . .

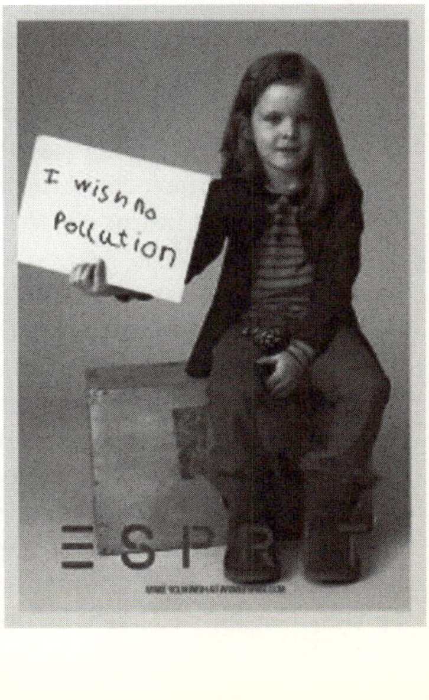

[11] See Pascal Gielen, 'The Hybrid Artist and Arts Education Beyond Art,' lecture at the University of the Arts Helsinki, March 15, 2016. *https://www.youtube.com/watch?v=VKFbXF0uNDc* See also 'De hybride kunstenaar' (The Hybrid Artist), research document (in Dutch) by C. van Winkel, P. Gielen and K. Zwaan, 2012.

[12] Archived website: *http://homeshopbeijing.org*

Unfortunately, HomeShop no longer exists. In the end, the challenges of working in a collective, the harsh reality of the urban environment of Beijing, the additional obstacles posed by working in a group consisting partially of expats, and the desire to build alternative value systems without being truly rooted in Beijing, all proved too much to handle. Ruangrupa, which faced similar challenges, did manage to survive and flourish, although there were some moments where it seemed it might not make it either.

Jakarta is a perfect illustration of the consequences of rapid urbanisation. I have been told that Jakarta is the city with the greatest number of shopping malls in the world. Residents and visitors alike go about their business under constant pressure of traffic jams, floods, litter, poor infrastructure, housing shortages, etc.

Beijing is a world capital shaped by the extremes of a new capitalist order, as well as by a complex mix of global and local customs, and a high degree of competitiveness in every imaginable professional sector. The shiny façade of modern-day China is a perfect metaphor not only for the excesses of globalisation, but also in a sense for the art world. Struggling to make yourself visible, having something of value to offer, simply exercising your profession are by no means obvious in a city with millions of residents and millions more pouring in from the countryside. Life here is all about dreams, exploitation, opportunism, ambitions, neglect, broken processes, ignorance, survival, hope… Beijing is no city for the naïve, and neither is Jakarta. Both are constantly confronting you with the extreme limits of your own ambitions, your own sincere intentions and your own shortcomings.

Ruangrupa began from the need for shared space, a house. HomeShop gradually developed as a meeting place for people with a variety of interests, a supportive structure based on the need to facilitate non-hierarchical, collaborative, non-macho art practices.

For both ruangrupa and HomeShop, projects are not based on intellectual concepts but on relating to the reality of the environment in which they are located. Projects that may on first sight seem local, that usually begin from the perspective of the local dimension, almost always sooner or later connect in some way to a global reality.

Why practical examples from the Far East?

– Our Western way of doing things, of thinking, acting and producing, are still tied to the perspective of a humanist, modernist way of seeing things. We must begin by recognising that this perspective is a European and Eurocentric one. Our actions, whether we think of ourselves as conservative or progressive, elitist or populist, will always be linked to this perspective.

– The typical contemporary art practice is part of a product-oriented society focused on overproduction,

Socially engaged art practices are not by definition also socially active practices. In Indonesia as well as in the West, there is a danger that the art market will exploit this theme in order to increase the appeal of artists, while for artists it can be tempting to present their art as a social practice, whether in the marketplace or as a tactic for acquiring funding.

'Supangkat (Important Indonesian artcritic) sheds a feeble light upon this discussion when he writes: "Several contemporary artists (painters) even entered the art market despite the fact that their works represent mostly social realities and are meant to have social impact. Contemporary art work, in contrast with the pleasant, beautiful mainstream paintings, is critical and political". It seems that Yogyakartan artists entered the art market not despite but because of their social and political subject matter. But what happens to the social and political "impact" of these works when they are commodified, consumed, and thereby exoticized? If their socio-political importance ever existed, does it only exist in the past? Is it proudly remembered as a nationalist urge for independence? Is it neutralized and forgotten in the present? Or is it merely an exotic representation, an export product, not much different from the colonial Beautiful Indies paintings, a contemporary form of political kitsch or political porn? There is no easy or straightforward answer to these questions. It may be clear that painting was as in fact a means for levelling critique in a context where direct political action was forbidden, censored and dangerous. However, it is clear that "political art" refers to the often-symbolic representation of "the political", be it by means of painting, drawing, installation, etc. Not only the terms "political" or "social" are in need of further definition, also the conventions around art need to

individual performance, personal success, etc. But what is the value of this personal success, if the only way to achieve it is to undermine our original intentions?

– The artistic discourse seems to have been comprehensively co-opted, as can be seen in the instrumentalisation and appropriation of the aesthetics of contemporary art by the real estate industry, the cultural industry, product branding, city branding, investors, politicians, etc. Artists in Beijing and Jakarta are confronted even more harshly with this reality than we are, usually due to the absence of an institutional tradition for contemporary art.

– It can be quite a challenge to find and claim your place in the midst of superficially similar activities; due to the huge gap between on one hand the alternative world of artists' initiatives, and on the other hand the commercial world of art collectors, members of ruangrupa often feel forced to present themselves on more commercial platforms.

– For a variety of reasons, Indonesian cultural and social activities often start from a sense of involvement with friends and neighbours, without too much concern at this stage for the conceptual content of the project.

– As I have said before, our Western way of doing things, of thinking, acting and producing, is stuck. It's not so much that there is a crisis of the social-democratic model; the crisis is rather one of our vision of individual acting. The nation state, the free market, and public institutions are all being thoroughly reconsidered and redeveloped. In the words of the postcolonial theorist Saeed Ur-Rehman:

> *'Modernity is generally defined as a secularizing social condition (Archetti, 1996) that produces a rationalized social sphere which, Max Weber has argued, is a distinguishing characteristic of the West (Weber, 1930: 24–7). Thus, the secularly rationalized social sphere and its Eurocentricity challenge non-western modes of knowing and being in the world. The contemporary conditions of knowledge production have become Eurocentric through the dominance of western modernity achieved through colonialist and imperialist practices, producing a westernization of knowledge production and meaning-making at a global level.'* [13]

By examining a number of Indonesian artists and artists' initiatives (besides ruangrupa, I will be discussing four

be reconsidered. Let us first look into the notion of "the political" as described by political theorist Chantal Mouffe and art critic Claire Bishop's concept of "relational antagonism".'

Sanne Oorthuizen, 'The Phoenix of Linear Time: Indonesian Contemporary Art and the Question of History' (MA thesis), 2012.

• • •

'Free as in free speech? Free as in free beer? Free as in free world? Free as in free markets? Free as in free labor? Using the word "free" is ambiguous as it can be used to celebrate the excesses of neoliberal capitalism and/or imply a confrontational position to this regime. It is important to clarify what we mean when we say "free". Who is free and what exactly are they free/freed from? Free is not always good and structure is not always bad (see The Tyranny of Structurelessness). Freedom and structure are not necessarily oppositional. As Deleuze and Guattari caution, "Never believe that a smooth space will suffice to save us." Freedom might not be such a great thing if it means, like anonymous [...] that collective action produces terrorism, renunciation of social responsibility and intolerance or, like free markets, that openness produces extreme social and economic inequality. Perhaps it is important to rethink our relation to freedom.'

Collaborative Futures, 'The Future of Collaboration', written collaboratively, 2010. http://collaborative-futures.org

• • •

[13] Saeed Ur-Rehman, 'Secular Knowledge versus Islamic Knowledge and Uncritical Intellectuality: The Work of Ziauddin Sardar', in: *Cultural Dynamics*, March 2002, Vol. 14, No. 1, pp. 65-80.

'We are divided from ourselves; We are divided from each other; We are divided from the planet; From this separation, those in power can justify oppression and supremacy and cite competition as the basis of not only their success but the driving force behind all life. In constructive opposition to this view, our movement presents the world with a story of connection, cooperation, and the commons. This is lived through daily practice of ownership and control over our own lives and institutions, as individuals in powerful community with each other.'

Cliff Martin, 'Democratize the Education System! Engaging the Youth in Cooperative Culture', Grassroots Economic Organizing (GEO), 2015. http://www.geo.coop/story/democratize-education-system

. . .

additional examples in chapter 3) I hope to clarify how a gLEAP practice manifests itself and what it stands for. gLEAP is not a label for a specific art practice, but rather a working method for distilling concrete actions from such a practice, while questioning our own choices and biases. As such it can be applied to different kinds of collective or individual practices.

I have said that artists should be able and willing to assume different roles in the production process: as specialist, assistant, implementer, manager, artist, audience, etc. An interesting metaphor in this respect, often cited by members of ruangrupa, is the 'total football' developed in the Netherlands in the 1970s, in which any player can assume any position in the field at any time.

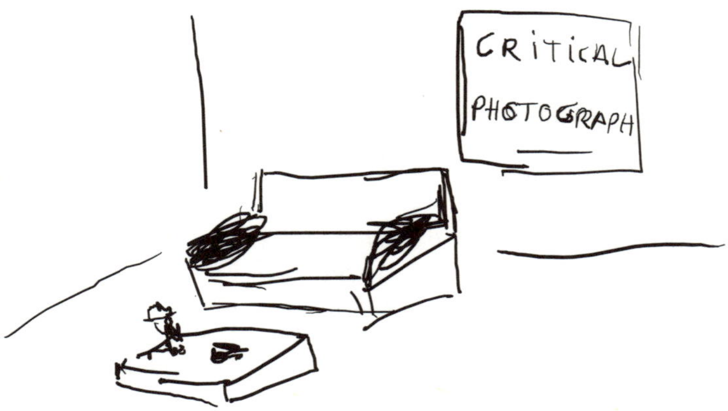

• IN PRACTICE
(≠ conceptual)

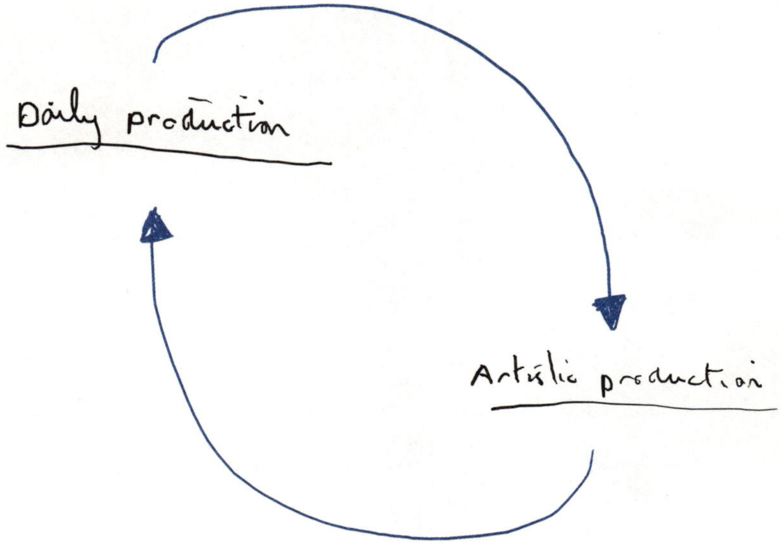

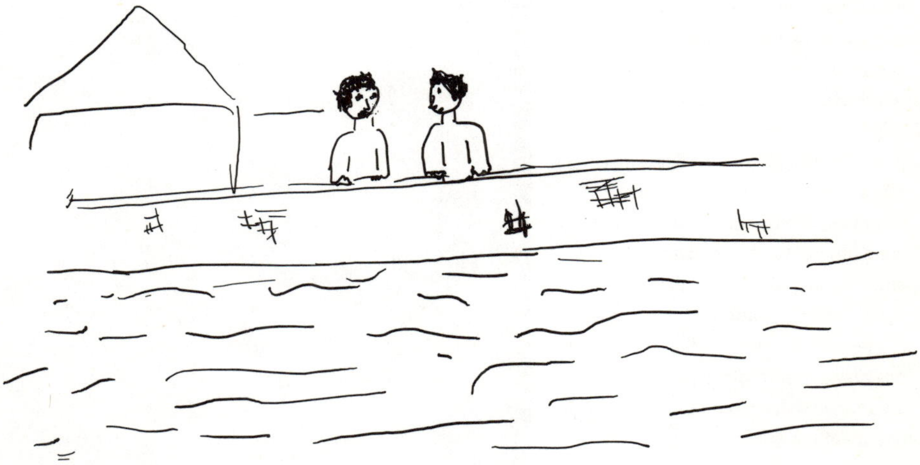

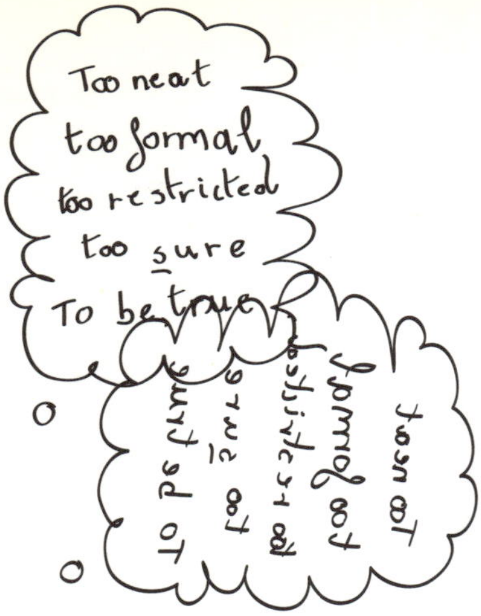

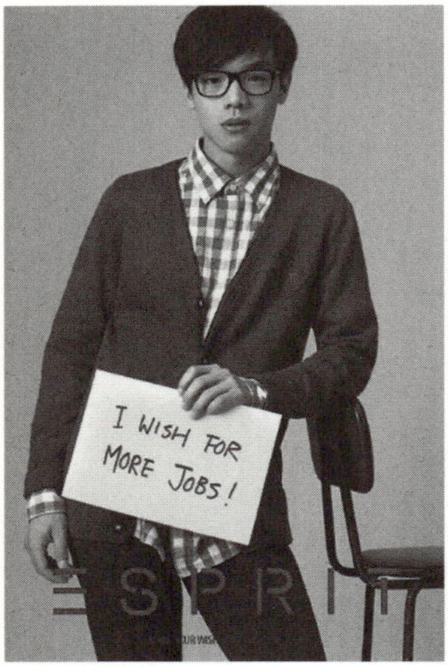

Has it become too easy to visually represent a subject? Are we being seduced by an artistic language in which we have believed for too long? The language (conceptual, aesthetic, poetic, underground, etc.) has long since been co-opted by politicians, investors, the fashion industry, sports conglomerates, the media industry and their like. Being or making something beautiful, intriguing, emerging, creative is no longer relevant. The time has come, not to make another project about toilet paper, but to never again use toilet paper…

Summary of a conversation between the Australian artist Michael Yuen and myself, Beijing, 2010.

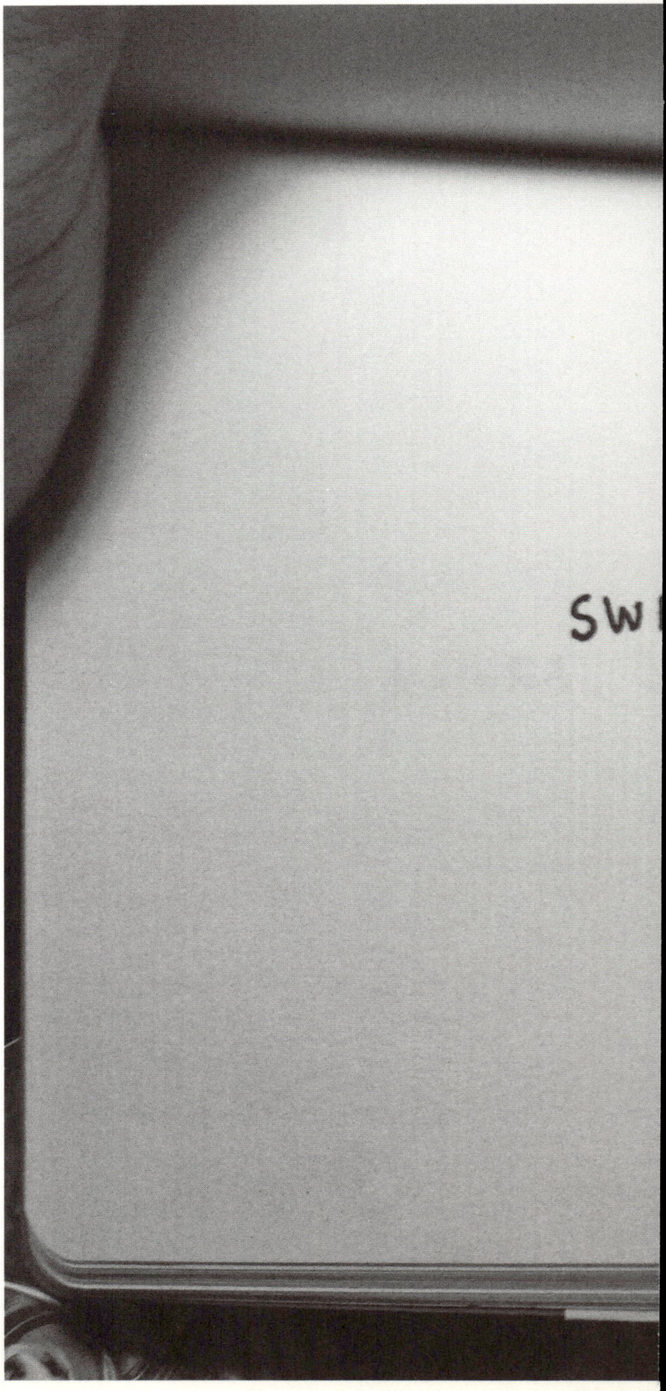

Insert to Chapter 1

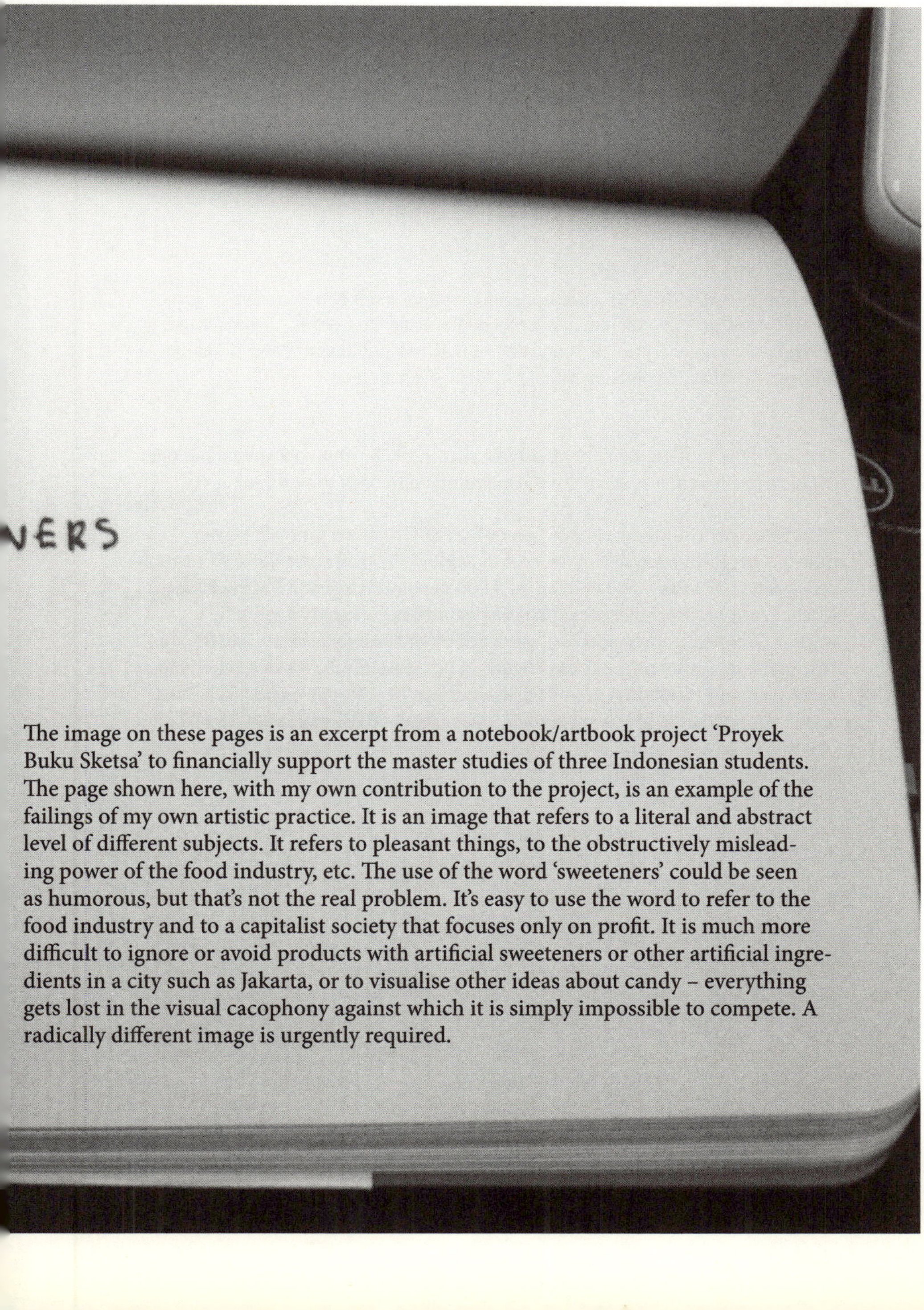

The image on these pages is an excerpt from a notebook/artbook project 'Proyek Buku Sketsa' to financially support the master studies of three Indonesian students. The page shown here, with my own contribution to the project, is an example of the failings of my own artistic practice. It is an image that refers to a literal and abstract level of different subjects. It refers to pleasant things, to the obstructively misleading power of the food industry, etc. The use of the word 'sweeteners' could be seen as humorous, but that's not the real problem. It's easy to use the word to refer to the food industry and to a capitalist society that focuses only on profit. It is much more difficult to ignore or avoid products with artificial sweeteners or other artificial ingredients in a city such as Jakarta, or to visualise other ideas about candy – everything gets lost in the visual cacophony against which it is simply impossible to compete. A radically different image is urgently required.

Zottegem 2013:

België, de grijze kolonie van Frankrijk

OPINIE – 31/07/13, 05u56
De commercialisering van onze ouderenzorg kent maar één winnaar: de grote commerciële groepen en hun aandeelhouders. Kurt De Loor is Vlaams Volksvertegenwoordiger (sp.a) en voorzitter van OCMW Zottegem dat een van de grootste openbare rusthuizen uitbaat in Oost-Vlaanderen.

Commerciële initiatiefnemers investeren niet in rusthuizen voor uw mooie ogen of uw grijze haren, laat staan om u een prettige oude dag te bezorgen

Het Franse bedrijf Medica koopt Senior Living Group, de grootste private uitbater van rusthuizen in België. Met de verkoop komen maar liefst 47 rusthuizen, goed voor ruim 5.500 bedden en 3.000 personeelsleden in Franse handen. Medica, een beursgenoteerde groep die rusthuizen in Frankrijk en Italië uitbaat, prijst de Belgische financieel 'veilige' markt voor rusthuisuitbaters aan bij zijn beleggers: de demografie evolueert gunstig en de Belgische sociale zekerheid komt voor 44 procent tussen in de prijs voor een bed. Ronduit onethisch. Niet alleen stroomt het geld van onze sociale zekerheid op die manier in de zakken van de Franse aandeelhouders, de betaalbaarheid en de toegankelijkheid van de hele ouderenzorgsector staat op het spel. Of willen we van onze rusthuizen een 'Electrabel bis' maken?
...

De Morgen 31/07/13

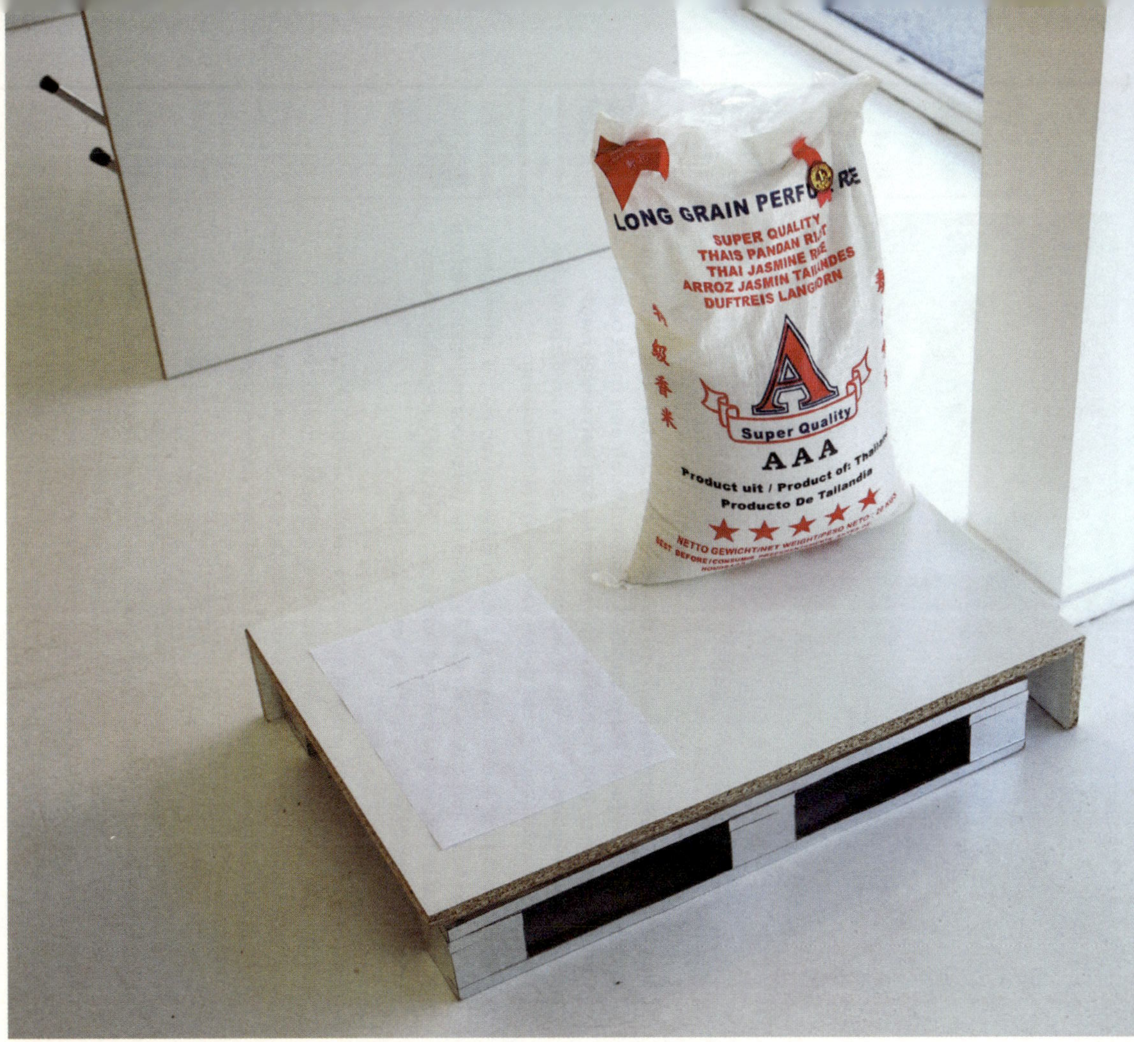

Gert Robijns, Wake & Sleep, 2013 – reinaart vanhoe, De gewone belegger moet beschermd worden, 2013

As part of his exhibition in the gallery White-Out Studio in Knokke-Heist, Belgium, the artist Gert Robijns invited a number of colleague artists to place an artwork upon his own artwork. I had the privilege of being one of those artists. My contribution addressed the topic of speculation on the financial value of food or artworks, and the role played by small investors and their money in this kind of speculation. Though I was pleased with my own contribution, I could imagine that most of the public may find it difficult to understand my intention with this artwork. Also, an important consideration was that my artwork could be sold to a private/institutional collector, so that I could use the money to support independent seed banks and independent farmers, thereby bypassing the middleman altogether. However in this sense the artwork by Paolo Cirio on the following page seems more focused and also more disruptive.

AD | NEDERLAND | BUITENLAND | SPORT | SHOW | REGIO

BUITENLAND

VN: een mobieltje is makkelijker te vinden dan een wc

Aanbevelen Delen 12 Tweet G+1 0

Bewerkt door: Redactie
22-3-13 - 05:32 bron: AP

BEWAAR ARTIKEL

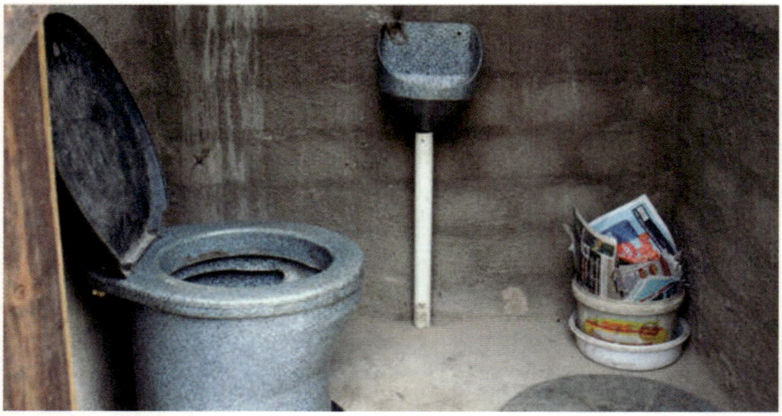

Wc in Durban, Zuid-Afrika © afp.

Van de zeven miljard mensen op de wereld beschikken zes miljard over een mobiele telefoon. Maar slecht 4,5 miljard heeft een toilet of een latrine. Met deze boodschap is de VN donderdag een wereldwijde campagne begonnen die moet leiden tot verbetering van de sanitaire omstandigheden voor grote delen van de wereldbevolking.

Plaatsvervangend secretaris-generaal Jan Eliassen van de VN spreekt van een 'stille ramp'. Het ontbreken van hygiënische wc's voor miljarden mensen bewijst dat er nog steeds extreme armoede is. Het toont volgens hem ook aan hoe groot de verschillen in de wereld nog zijn.

Volgens de VN doet 15 procent van de wereldbevolking (1,1 miljard mensen) zijn ontlasting buiten of in ruimten waar geen enkele hygiënische maatregelen zijn genomen. Het is een van de grootste oorzaken van diarree, die elk jaar de dood veroorzaakt van 750 duizend kinderen van vier jaar en jonger.

De praktijk van 'open ontlasting' zou in 2025 helemaal moeten zijn verdwenen, aldus Eliassen. Wereldleiders moetetn daarvoor meer actie ondernemen, zegt hij. Op een top in 2000 was dit een van de zogeheten Millennium Development Goals. De VN meent dat er maar weinig van de plannen terechtkomt.

MEER OVI
VERENIG
ONTWIKI

AD NI
20:10 Ma
18:43 'Ru
18:19 Tu
18:16 Tw
15:38 'Ba
FOTOSP
FOTOSP

AD PO
Woedenc af (35998x
Australis af dankzi
Restaura serveerd (20792x ge
'Badr Hai mishande

Zoek i

'Loophole for All'
https://www.youtube.com/watch?v=BLtFrWJ-EZk

Loophole for All, an artwork by Paolo Cirio

'This artwork unveiled over 200000 Cayman Islands companies and reversed global finance machination to serve a creative agenda. The website Loophole4All.com promoted the sale of real identities of anonymous Cayman companies at low cost to democratize the privileges of offshore businesses by forging Certificates of Incorporation documents for each company, all issued with the artist's real name and signature. This performance generated international media attention, engaged an active audience and drew outrage from authorities on the Cayman Islands, international law and accounting firms, PayPal, and real owners of the companies. Further, the artist interviewed major experts and produced a video documentary investigating offshore centers to expose their social costs and to envision solutions to global economic inequality. In the offline art installation, the paper trail of the project is displayed with prints of the counterfeited Certificates of Incorporation and the documents of the scheme set up for the operation.'

Paolo Cirio, 'Loophole for All', project description on the artist's website. *https://www.paolocirio.net/work/loophole-for-all/*

This artwork may not be obviously or completely recognisable as an artwork, or may be exhibited in an awkward way, but that's not the most important point here. In this artwork, Paolo Cirio is able to show his subject on a number of different levels. He not only refers to specific mechanisms but also takes the trouble to actively incorporate these mechanisms in his artwork, rather than merely making them the subject of an intellectual exercise.

Niceism

'Nice-ism n. tendency, more or less socially codified, to approach reality in terms of whether others behave cordially; tyranny of decorum which disallows thinking or acting for oneself; mode of interaction based upon the above absence of critical judgement or autonomy.

All of us prefer what is friendly, sincere, pleasant-nice. But in an immiserated world of pervasive and real crisis, which should be causing all of us to radically reassess everything, the nice can be the false.

The face of domination is often a smiling one, a cultured one. Auschwitz comes to mind, with its managers who enjoyed their Goethe and Mozart. Similarly, it was not evil-looking monsters who built the A-bomb but nice liberal intellectuals. Ditto regarding those who are computerizing life and those who in other ways are the mainstays of participation in this rotting order, just as it is the nice businessperson (self-managed or otherwise) who is the backbone of a cruel work-and-shop existence by concealing it's real horrors.

Cases of niceism include the peaceniks, whose ethic of niceness puts them – again and again and again – in stupid ritualized, no-win situations, those Earth First!ers who refuse to confront the thoroughly reprehensible ideology at the top of "their" organization, and Fifth Estate, whose highly important contributions now seem to be in danger of an eclipse by liberalism. All the single-issue causes, from ecologism to feminism, and all the militancy in their service, are only ways of evading the necessity of a qualitative break with more than just the excesses of the system.

The nice as the perfect enemy of tactical or analytical thinking: Be agreeable; don't let having radical ideas make waves in your personal behavior. Accept the pre-packaged methods and limits of the daily strangulation. Ingrained deference, the conditioned response to "play by the rules" – authority's rules – this is the real Fifth Column, the one within us.

In the context of a mauled social life that demands the drastic as a minimum response toward health, niceism becomes more and more infantile, conformist and dangerous. It cannot grant joy, only more routine and isolation. The pleasure of authenticity exists only against the grain of society. Niceism keeps us all in our places, confusedly reproducing all that we supposedly abhor. Let's stop being nice to this nightmare and all who would keep us in it.'

John Zerzan, The Nihilist's Dictionary, 1994.

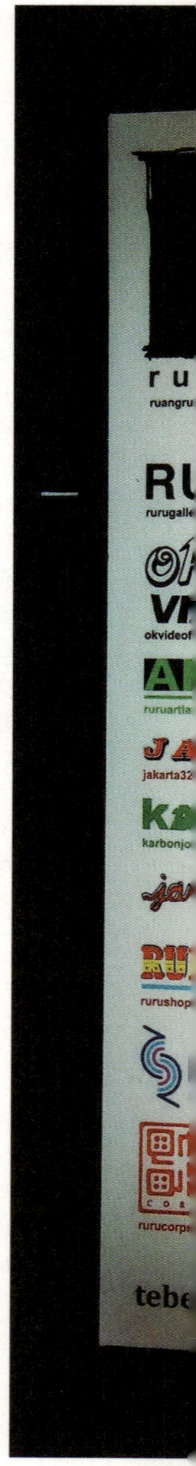

Chapter 2:

Ruangrupa, an artists' initiative from Jakarta, Indonesia

Art as organisation, art in the context of other social activities (= inventiveness).

In this chapter I will be presenting the findings of my research of ruangrupa.[1] What are some of its typical characteristics, how does it deploy its activities, and how does this relate to my attempt at formulating a '(g)Locally Embedded Art Practice' (gLEAP)?[2]

I would like to begin with a quotation on anarchism by the anthropologist and activist Jeffrey S. Juris, which I find particularly relevant to the working ethic I have encountered within ruangrupa, as well as the position they envision for themselves within their social environment:

> *'Anarchists fervently believe in local autonomy and self-management, as Colin Ward (1973: 58) explains: "The anarchist conclusion is that every kind of human activity should begin from what is local and immediate." As a result, according to Voline: "True emancipation can only be brought about by the direct action of those concerned... and not under the banner of any political party or ideological body. Their emancipation must be based in concrete action and 'self-administration' " (quoted in Guérin 1970: 37). In this sense, anarchist praxis means acting on behalf of one's own group or community, rather than another (Franks 2003). In contrast to representative democracy, Kropotkin (in Raymond 1999) thus promoted a mode of political organization that is closer to self-government, to government "of oneself by oneself." This does not necessarily mean that larger associations are never justified, but rather that these should always be based on local needs and autonomy.'* [3]

We may well ask ourselves to what extent this European perspective can be applied in the case of ruangrupa. Members of ruangrupa often refer to anarchism, but the question remains to what degree the characteristics described in the quotation above can be said to apply to ruangrupa.[4]

---

1 *'It is important to note the way many of ruangrupa's activities over the past ten years can be linked to the collective's name, which combines the Indonesian term for "a space" (ruang) and its (outward) "appearance" or "visualisation" (rupa); the name hence denotes a "visual space", or rather a visualspace within the context of Jakarta. Merging the two terms for the visual and for space realises a close interdependence in which the appearance of an actual space generates a three-dimensional realm in which objects transpire and events occur, and whereby its (outward) appearance as a space is at once realised through visual means.'* Thomas J. Berghuis, 'Ruangrupa', in: *Third Text*, Vol. 25, Issue 4, 2011, pp. 395-407.

2 See chapter 3, particularly section 3.6.1, for a detailed of definition of gLEAP.

3 Jeffrey S. Juris, 'Anarchism, or the Cultural Logic of Networking', in: Amster et al. (eds.), *Contemporary Anarchist Studies: An Introductory Anthology of Anarchy in the Academy*, Routledge, 2009.

4 For an interesting perspective of how ruangrupa understands anarchism, see the 7th Freedom Lecture, 2014 by Ade Darmawan, organised by the political and cultural centre

2.1 What is ruangrupa?

Ruangrupa is a house: 24 hours a day, 7 days a week.

- Working on an artistic/cultural practice from the basis of a house.
- Connecting and strengthening local and international networks.
- Working from the perspective of an urban youth culture,[5] and within an urban infrastructure.

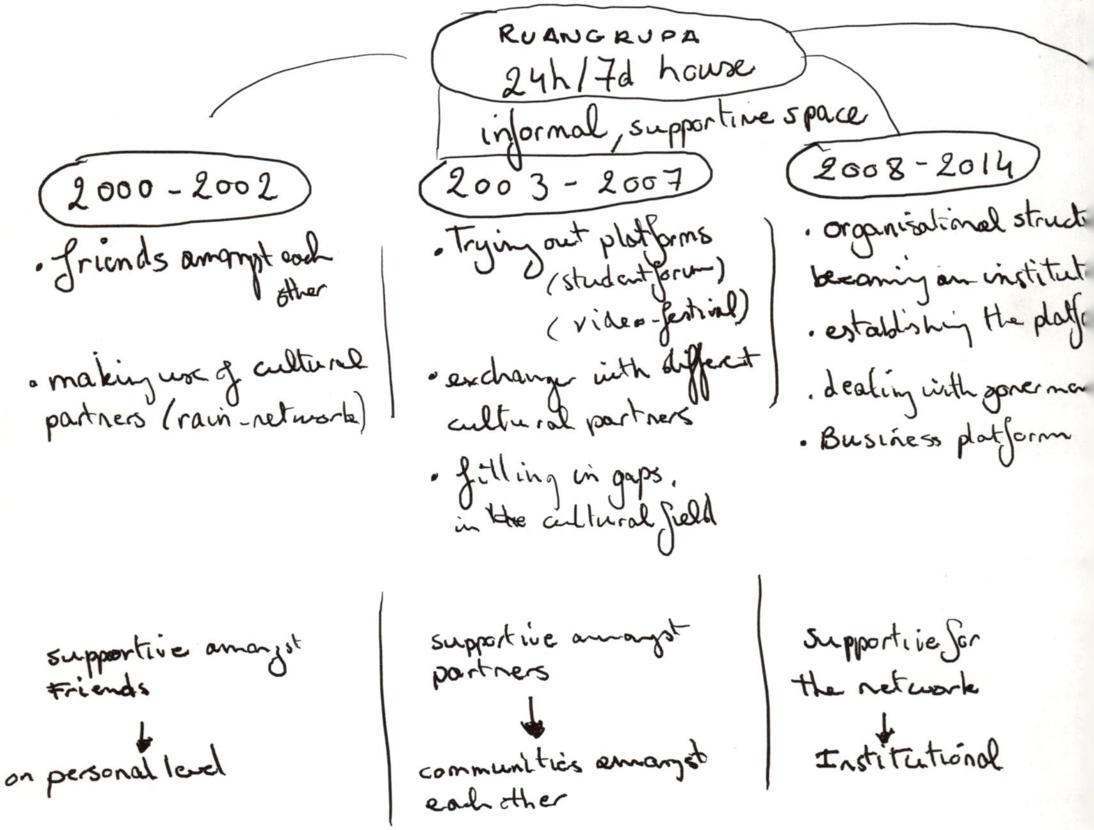

De Balie (Amsterdam) in collaboration with Amnesty International; a video of the lecture can be seen on De Balie's Vimeo page: *https://vimeo.com/109858418*

5 *'Youth and students played an important role in the demise of Soeharto's New Order. During the reformasi, youth culture was given previously denied freedoms, and allowed to question things previously taken for granted. Writing about ruangrupa is writing about a youth movement.'* Nuraini Juliastuti, 'Ruangrupa: A Conversation on Horizontal Organisation', in: *Afterall*, No. 30, Summer 2012.

Mirwan Andan, a member of ruangrupa since 2010, once described the collective as follows:

> *'Ruangrupa is an initiative established in Jakarta by a group of artists; it is a non-profit organization aimed at promoting the progress of ideas in visual arts in the urban context and the wider cultural sphere through exhibitions, festivals, visual art laboratories, workshops, research, and journal publications. In early 2000, ruangrupa was founded by people who were educated in Institut Kesenian Jakarta (Jakarta Arts Institute), Institut Seni Indonesia (Indonesian Arts Institute), and the Rijksakademie van Beeldende Kunsten, Amsterdam. Soon afterwards ruangrupa started to organize regular discussions to elaborate a variety of issues and problems pertaining to contemporary arts and their relation to the city space. The founders believed that in the context of Jakarta, it was necessary to have a group that explores issues of urban and public space by using visual arts as the main medium and involving young people as its actors. Based on this perspective, ruangrupa designed a number of art projects participated in by young artists from Indonesia and abroad. These projects, involving various forms of media such as graphic design, video/ film, photography, installation, performance art, murals, graffiti, sound art, paintings, drawings, posters, t-shirts, comics, zines, objects and mixed media were organized in events or programs; some are held regularly, such as the artist residency program, The Jakarta International Video Festival and regular exhibitions at the RURU Gallery. In addition to running internal programs, ruangrupa has been invited many times to participate in international events in order to present narratives about Jakarta (in particular) or Indonesia (generally) through visual art projects. One such event that needs to be mentioned is the Istanbul Biennial, Turkey, in 2005, where ruangrupa presented the figure of Benyamin Sueb as an icon that represents lowermiddle class identity in Jakarta, connecting it with Turkish symbol of the lower-middle class Kema Sunal. In terms of composition, at first the people involved in ruangrupa were limited to those with a visual art background, but later, people with diverse backgrounds such as architecture, literature, politics, international relations, sociology, anthropology, history, and communications were also invited to participate. Ruangrupa, which from the beginning was established and designed as a project of contemporary culture, tends to base its art projects on experimental research. As a result, multi-disciplinary perspectives later contributed to the initial projects as well as allowing for more enriching collaborations between disciplines. The close proximity between ruangrupa and youth culture in Jakarta, whose activities revolve around music (especially independent label),street art, and other forms of activities has assigned ruangrupa a specific audience to today. Urban youth culture, with its enthusiasm over experiments and crowds, has always been the audience of ruangrupa's programs. In some art projects, youth groups are specifically involved as actors in producing and distributing knowledge.'*[6]

6 Mirwan Andan, 'All for Jakarta – a note on the tenth anniversary of ruangrupa: Decompression #10, Expanding the Space and Public', in: *Inter-Asia Cultural Studies*, Vol. 12, Issue 4, 2011, pp. 591-602.

The ruangrupa house has developed throughout the years from a place for facilitating the development of artistic practices within a small circle of friends, to a broader platform for various elements within the socio-cultural sector on a municipal, regional, national and international level. As I described in chapter 1, the city of Jakarta which provides the everyday context for ruangrupa is such an overwhelming environment that a contextually logical connection with this environment becomes more or less inevitable.

Activities do not arise from the lofty perspective of the artist's studio, but from the everyday reality of the city. The practice relates to the true fictions[7] of the city, and much less to the fictions of an artist's studio.

The necessity of achieving results, of understanding the urban environment and of defining one's relationship with this environment, means that ruangrupa does not have the luxury of working from a distant or contemplative perspective. Instead, artists must get their hands dirty, experience the environment firsthand:

> *'See and react upon what is going on. React upon it by deriving projects, interfering in situations, getting involved with government, etc. Play to understand, to see, to get involved, to understand your engagement, etc.'* [8]

2.2 How does ruangrupa function?

In the following section I will be examining a number of ruangrupa's programmatic components and their specific characteristics in relation to a '(g)Locally Embedded Art Practice' (gLEAP). Then I will be examining in detail the organisational structure of ruangrupa.

2.2.1 Origins

> *'We needed indie music to become different (we watched movies like Lost Highway, Suburbia, Trainspotting, Basquiat, on VCD. The Suharto regime didn't care about piracy. Music (dangdut jaipong, indie, punk, etc.) and film functioned as a gateway, as activist material.'*
> *From a conversation with some ruangrupa members, June 2014.*

The roots of ruangrupa can be traced to the Indonesian indie (independent) music scene of sometime around 1995. From the activities taking place within this scene, particularly in the major cities of Jakarta and Yogyakarta, a cultural network emerged which was for and by youth. Indie music offered an alternative worldview and can in that context be compared to the punk movement in Europe.[9] However it is far from certain whether this indie movement also had an activist component. The emphasis was rather on speaking up for other forms of expression than what was offered at art schools and universities. This all took place during the last years and days of the 31-year Suharto dictatorship. The youth culture consisted to a great extent of people from the 'lower' socio-economic classes, who were not interested in politics or institutional programmes.

---

7 Fictions should be understood here as real-life options, inventive also-solutions for organising and giving shape to situations in our everyday environments. Ruangrupa understands fiction (another more or less equivalent term would be speculation) as the inventiveness of individuals in a city such as Jakarta, also-possible realities which often turn out to be more interesting or thought-provoking than the fictitious representations of, say, a painting made in an artist's studio (see also section 2.3.3.1, 'Collective memory')

8 I have summarised and paraphrased here a conversation between the artist Irwan Ahmett and myself, November 2013.

9 *'In those days, the New Order stranglehold on media was just beginning to let up. Content was still closely monitored by the Ministry of Information, and just about everything else on TVRI was crushingly, almost painfully saccharine, inflated with government propaganda and Pancasila optimism. Nirvana, the Seattle grunge rockers, with their stripped-down aesthetic, torn jeans and gruff disdain for pop culture conventionality, were a breath of fresh air. "Just imagine", David said to me, as we chatted in his Jakarta recording studio a mile or so south of the Blok M shopping complex. "What happened in '91 in Indonesia was probably a lot like what happened in the Western world in '77, you know, the punk explosion."'* David Taringan, quoted in Brent Luvaas, 'The Indie Takeover', in: *Inside Indonesia*, No. 95, January-March 2009. *http://www.insideindonesia.org/the-indie-takeover*

Ruangrupa uses the language of youth, in other words: accessible, irreverent, playful. Also, supporting and building a community is a main characteristic of many communities in Indonesia, and thus also for artists and artists' initiatives. Another important daily reality of ruangrupa is related to the absence of government funding or other similar subsidies. Indonesian communities must rely on self-organisation of activities, acquiring knowledge independently, and setting up platforms by themselves.

In contrast to the West, where it is fashionable to be critical of institutionalisation, and where institutions that rely on public funding are endlessly confronted with populist political policies that seek to limit their breathing space,[10] in Indonesia there is on the contrary a certain need or even a longing for institutions. This could provide an interesting potential for cultural exchange, a dialogue on how institutions function and how they can be organised.[11] Also, since ruangrupa's very existence has much to do with issues such as these, it makes sense to examine the collective from this perspective as well.

2.2.2 Ruangrupa's activities and platforms, an introduction

During the course of its existence, ruangrupa has grown from an informal group of young artists living in a house, to an organisation with some 35 staff members and a variety of platforms. On the following page I have sketched ruangrupa's organisational structure, highlighting a number of ruangrupa's platforms in order to provide some insight into the practical functioning of the organisation. For a detailed description of these platforms and activities, see the first insert to the present chapter.

- Ruangrupa as an internationally operating artists' collective. In this context I have examined ruangrupa's contributions to the 2005 Istanbul Biennial and to the 2012-2013 Asia Pacific Triennial of Contemporary Art in Brisbane, Australia.
- OK. Video: a platform for audio-visual and digital production and presentation.
- Jakarta 32°C: a student biennale, for students from the city's various universities.
- Stiker Kota: a book focusing on popular visual culture and urban printing in the city, specifically sticker culture.
- RURU Gallery, a platform for young emerging artists/curators/writers, where presentations, exhibitions, workshops, publications, discussions, performances, etc., take place.
- Ruangrupa as an educative platform: ruangrupa is planning to start its own educational institute (though I must admit to wondering whether this is really necessary, and whether educational activities are not already sufficiently provided through existing programmes).

---

10 In Western countries such as the Netherlands, cultural policy nowadays is largely determined by linking the concept of cultural entrepreneurship to economic output (this ideology of 'creative industries' was first introduced in the United Kingdom by the new Labour government of Tony Blair, more specifically by Chris Smith, then Secretary of State for Culture, Media and Sport; it was quickly picked up by other social-liberal governments and policymakers such as Rick van der Ploeg in the Netherlands). In this perspective, art is expected to compete on the marketplace, more or less like any other commercial venture. This is ultimately a conservative worldview (focused on maintaining the status quo) in which words such as 'creative' or 'innovative', carry little more than symbolic value; though in the case of ostensibly centre-left politicians such as Smith and Van der Ploeg, there was at least some kind of vision focused on reaching a broader audience and promoting cultural diversity.

11 *'In my position at The Showroom I have to organise in a structured way, but at the same time I also have to make room for openness, for things to take their own course and have their own life. I worked in a bigger institution in the UK where the structure was so rigid that everything had to fit into it and there was no room for anything to be responsive, or for feedback to occur between the organisation and what it was producing. Here in Indonesia it has been interesting to see how and where these kinds of tensions occur, if at all. Many of the organisations we met seem to have evolved through friendship and have then become more formalised at certain points, often in order to accept funding. A lot of that funding comes from outside, so I'm interested in how you continue to do what you do without having to respond to outside agendas.' Emily Pethick, quoted in:* 'Toilet Tissue and Other Formless Organisational Matters', excerpt from a conversation between Antariksa (KUNCI, Yogyakarta), Binna Choi (Casco, Utrecht), Syafiatudina (KUNCI), Emily Pethick (The Showroom, London), and Ferdiansyah Thajib (KUNCI), January 31, 2015, KUNCI Cultural Studies Center, Yogyakarta, transcription by Edwinna Brennan. *http://openengagement.info/tag/the-showroom/*

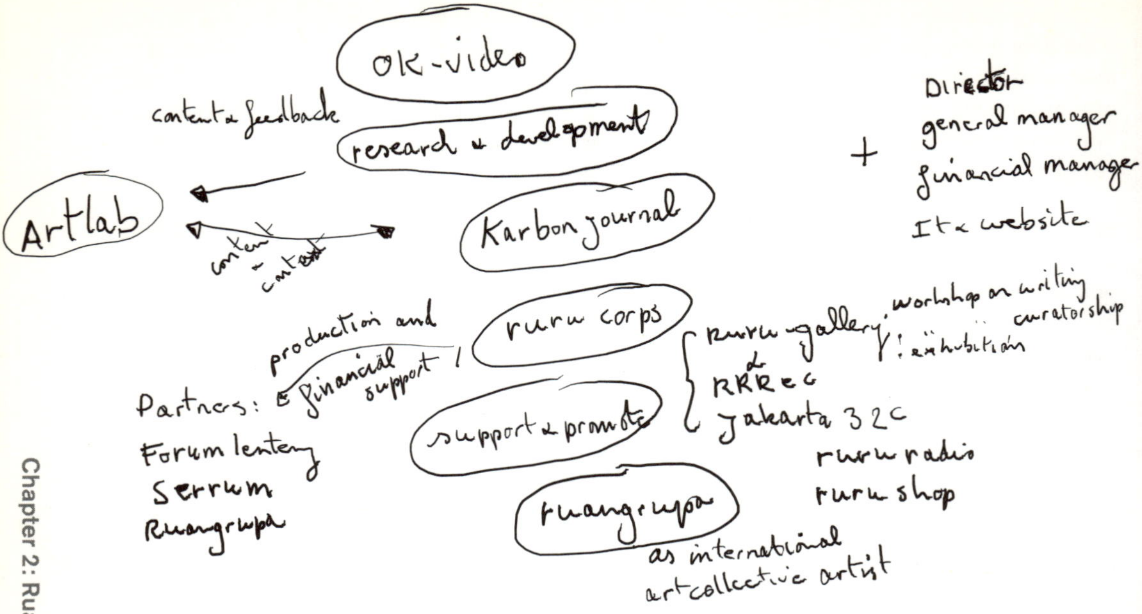

2.2.3 Some basic characteristics of ruangrupa

2.2.3.1 Specific to ruangrupa

I would like to start by mentioning three key characteristics which I believe are also the foundation of my interest in and involvement with ruangrupa.

Nongkrong: Nongkrong is a typically Indonesian concept or custom (see also the following section, 2.2.3.2, 'Indonesian customs that have shaped ruangrupa') that also happens to be crucial to how ruangrupa operates.[12] Nongkrong can be loosely translated as chatting, informal conversations not focused on a specific goal.[13] For ruangrupa, it is an essential method for collectively addressing topics without the need to immediately develop a concrete plan. Topics of conversation include humorous anecdotes, themes from social media and computer games, and everyday experiences of city life (a taxi ride, an encounter with a street vendor, family affairs, renting a house, etc.). These conversations may or may not lead to plans, which in turn may or may not end up being implemented in practice, all depending on a number of circumstances: a sudden momentum, an invitation, a sense of urgency, someone undertaking action, an annual plan for acquiring financing, etc.[14]

---

12 *'Walking into the Ruangrupa headquarters in a converted house in the middle of an inner city suburb, one's first indelible impression is of a group of people who do not seem to be doing very much of anything. People wander in and out of a slightly ramshackle space, conversation floats over tea and snacks, people tinker on laptops in an enervating fog of humidity. The contradiction between what Ruangrupa looks and feels like and the scope and professionalism of what it actually does is an abiding impression during my stay, one which is confirmed by other visitors. It is a refreshing contrast to the Johannesburg contemporary arts scene, where it can sometimes seem as though we are all insanely busy with generating "a lot of nothing", as an astute friend likes to put it.'* Joseph Gaylard, 'A Joburger in Jakarta: Notes on Ruangrupa and the Art of the Network', Visual Arts Network of South Africa, 2010. *http://vansa.co.za/about/copy_of_news/a-joburger-in-jakarta-notes-on-ruangrupa-and-the-art-of-the-network*

13 *'What is it with Indonesians (especially the young generation) that we love to nongkrong so much? Before you judge me, I'm not saying that nongkrong is bad – it's probably one of the most important reasons why I chose to come back to Indonesia.'* Tasa Nugraza Barley, 'View Point: How 'nongkrong' is part of our culture', in: *The Jakarta Post*, January 20, 2009.

14 One could also say that the international activist network Anonymous arose and functions in a similar way:

Ruangrupa's working rhythm: The working rhythm has two speeds. Things will carry on slowly and in an unstructured way for a while, and then once in a while there will be a peak of activity in which things suddenly take on a tangible form. A project then becomes an occasion for further development, and becomes part of a larger stream, an ongoing flux with intermediate public moments. These moments are not unimportant and are also the focus of a great deal of energy, but always in relation to the flow. It is important to pass on and absorb knowledge, and thus to be a place for production of various moments, always with a focus on one's own particular location, in this case the urban living environment of Jakarta.

Formal and informal structure: For ruangrupa, it's not a problem that everyone has their own way of working, however impractical this may often be. There's plenty of room for the idiosyncrasies of all members, who also all have their own responsibilities. There's an unspoken sense of mutual trust or acceptance; conflicts are simply part of the flow, challenges to be overcome. This does mean that some members, particularly the younger ones, occupy a more fragile position within the collective. Ruangrupa works with an understanding that each member's own preferences or wishes are always part of a broader whole. The partial surrender of your own preferences is important in order to be able to get things done, and this also brings you one step further toward getting a grip on your environment. It's a mix between on one hand following your own path, and on the other hand integrating this path within a larger collective flow. Ruangrupa focuses on the environment of things, rather than on isolated needs or wishes. An understanding of 'being with' (Heidegger)[15] as the basis of one's own artistic practice. This does mean that you will often need to keep on pressing your own agenda in order to ensure that the topics that are important to you continue to receive the attention you feel they deserve.

2.2.3.2 Indonesian customs that have shaped ruangrupa

Establishing and maintaining collaborative platforms is a natural practice within Indonesian society, and thus by extension within ruangrupa. People know from experience that they have to organise things themselves, that there is no point in waiting for the government to solve your problems. The concepts we will be examining in this section are by no means merely theoretical, but are in fact an intrinsic part of the fabric of all (everyday, working and artistic) activities.

It is also useful to remember that a number of social concepts have become contaminated by the Suharto dictatorship, and may thus have different connotations in different situations. In some cases there are contradictory definitions or understandings as to the origins of a concept.[16]

We can observe here a complex system of implicit and explicit values which are fundamental to the practice of ruangrupa and other related initiatives in Indonesia. The contrast with the model of individual market-driven artistic practice as we understand it in the West is striking.

A number of these concepts will be referred to at later moments in the text.

'The majority of Anonymous' activity is visible only to Anonymous. The members trade images and jokes between one another on 4chan and other sites. They traffic in pornography, shock imagery, and inane jokes. They collect and distribute the oddities of the web. However, Anonymous is also responsible for occasional external, organized actions – ranging from pranks done "for the lulz", to large scale activist projects. The most visible and longest lived of such projects is called Project Chanology, and is a large scale, distributed war on The Church of Scientology.' CollaborativeFutures, 'Anonymous', in: *CollaborativeFutures Book Sprint*, 2010. *http://write.flossmanuals.net/collaborativefutures/anonymous/*

15 William Cornwell, 'Making Sense of the Other: Husserl, Carnap, Heidegger, and Wittgenstein', paper presented at the 20th World Congress of Philosophy, Boston, August 10-15, 1998.

16 See for example Benedict Richard O'Gorman Anderson, *Language and Power: Exploring Political Cultures in Indonesia*, Cornell University Press, 1990, p. 148.

Gotong royong: Communal self-help, building things together, collectively supporting each other without expecting a favour in return. For example, maintaining collective spaces or buildings, organising funerals, cooperatively repairing houses after a flood.[17] [18]

KKN students (Kuliah Kerja Nyata): Until quite recently, students in Yogyakarta were required to perform a three-month internship (during the vacation period) in a village community. *'The underlying philosophy of the program is that university students are a privileged minority who have an obligation to "give something back to the community" at the conclusion of their studies.'* [19]

Sanggar: An (artist's) sanggar is a traditional meeting place where apprentices can meet and learn from masters, without specific rules or obligations, and from there they can develop their own practice ('cari sendiri' = finding your own way). Sanggars can be seen as informal places for education. An important principle of the sanggar is that the artist's task and responsibility is always to focus on the people (individual and collective). The artist draws energy and insight from the community's activities, experiences, etc. These insights and observations can then be worked out in the artist's studio. Though the term Sanggar is often associated with the Sukarno[20] years, there seems to be no consensus on the precise origin of the word. Since the Suharto years, the term has clearly taken on a more negative connotation.

Mushawarah and *mufakat*: These two concepts find their origins in political activity. 'Mushawarah' means an agreement reached between heads of villages. The consultations leading to such an agreement, which can go on for days, focus on sharing ideas and opinions and eventually achieving a 'mufakat' or consensus.

Guyup (or *guyub) santoso*: Working collaboratively toward a greater common welfare.

Patungah: A crowdfunding of sorts; raising money, often for a common interest. Jatiwangi Art Factory (see chapter 3, section 3.3.2, 'Practitioners', collective Jatiwangi Art Factory) often works according to this principle by requesting contributions in the form of materials, food, labour, etc. They can do this partially because they are deeply rooted in the culture of their village; in this sense this also relates to the idea of to 'gotong royong'.

Warga: Literally means 'people' but in practice often means citizens or citizenship, people together.

Turba: A somewhat contentious term that has become contaminated by recent history. It literally means going back to one's roots. The term gained negative connotations during the Suharto dictatorship. There seems to be no general agreement as to the exact origins of the term; some people told me it originated during the Sukarno years, others said it had been around long before that.

---

17 *'Gotong royong is a very familiar social concept in many parts of Indonesia and forms one of the core tenets of Indonesian philosophy.'* Sharlene Furuto, *Social Welfare in East Asia and the Pacific, Columbia University Press, 2013, p.149.*

18 Koentjaraningrat, *Gotong Rojong: Some Social-Anthropological Observations on Practices in Two Villages of Central Java*, Equinox, 2009.

19 Source: Australian Consortium for 'In-Country' Indonesian Studies, *http://www.acicis.murdoch.edu.au/hi/dsip2.html*

20 Sukarno was the leader of the Indonesian struggle for independence from the Netherlands immediately following World War II. He then became the first president of Indonesia. During the final years of his rule, Sukarno followed an increasingly left-wing course, until he was deposed in 1967 by one of his generals, Suharto, who would go on to rule the country in an autocratic fashion for 31 years.

2.3 Characteristics of ruangrupa

'The artist profession is not one that distances itself from the public and social reality. We believe, for example, that there are many ways to deal with global capitalism. One can try to grasp global capitalism in the other continent and transform it on canvas through abstract painting. One can also deal with it by expressing it through mundane, day-to-day expressions, which can surprise and inspire people to think critically at the way things are. Ruangrupa is not unconscious that global capitalism has long been an octopus lurking in the bedroom, but one needs to deal with it not only by grand projects, but rather, once again, with small narratives with more frequency.'
Mirwan Andan, 'All for Jakarta – a note on the tenth anniversary of ruangrupa: Decompression #10, Expanding the Space and Public', in: Inter-Asia Cultural Studies, Vol. 12, Issue 4, 2011, pp. 591-602.

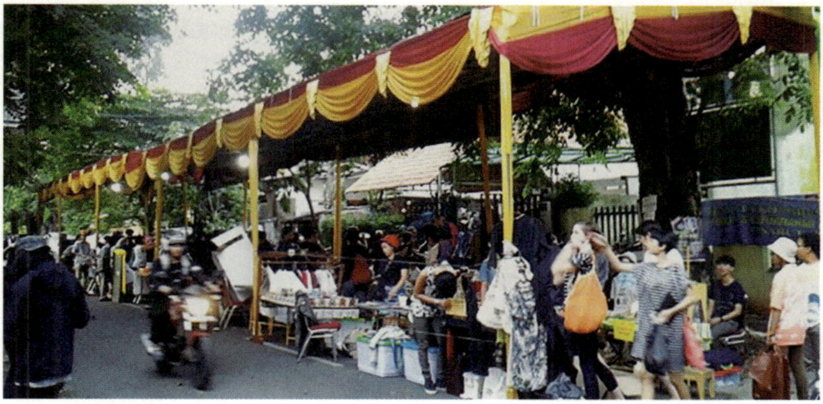

2.3.1 Facilitary structures

2.3.1.1 Supportive structure

Providing practical and theoretical support to each other's collective or individual artistic goals.

Various plans are implemented without the need for you to be the leading force behind the ideas. You support people from your environment, people you care for, people you value and appreciate. You are able to see and think beyond your own ideas, particularly on a practical level. The 'genius' of the individual artist (assuming such a thing even exists) is less important than the broader flow of ideas and implementations.

For example, Hafiz Rancajale, one of the founding members of ruangrupa, was able to develop his interest in film and video art; Reza Afisina, who has been a member since 2001, found in ruangrupa a suitable platform for developing his interest in the medium of performance.

2.3.1.2 Generous structure

Generous, open-minded sharing of knowledge and energy within our everyday and professional environment.

A generous structure offers an alternative to a calculating world, a mainstream world, a world in which we only offer our time and energy with a specific goal in mind.

The educational aspect within ruangrupa, and the possibility of simply hanging around, engaging in informal conversations ('nongkrong') can be seen as a 'continuous generous structure'.

The early years of ruangrupa were characterised by an intrinsically generous structure, if only because everything still needed to be built up. However it is becoming increasingly challenging to be generous with a full agenda. The current situation of ruangrupa is very energy-consuming, which has a negative effect on individuals, collaborative partners and collaborative efforts (see section 2.4.1, 'The necessity of doing too much').

One possible solution for retaining or reintroducing this generous structure is to reorganise (or to regenerate[21]). Because of its long-term presence and commitment within the cultural infrastructure of Jakarta, ruangrupa can also become a generous structure on a political level, by promoting the collective needs and wishes of its members and colleagues within the political agenda. Otherwise ruangrupa runs the risk of becoming just another cultural institution that merely refers to its social environment in its activities, but does not work with this environment – which is exactly what has happened to so many cultural institutions in the West.

- **Being mutually supportive is an essential element of the structure and fabric of ruangrupa. As Ade Darmawan, one of ruangrupa's founding members and its current director, once told me: often no one even seems to remember who exactly came up with what idea.**
- **Being generous also means on a very simple level being available: the ruangrupa house is open 24/7, you can always sleep there, you can always find someone to talk to, the library is open without restrictions. Spaces that are not currently being used can be claimed by anyone for working, sleeping, holding a meeting, etc. Programmes such as the RURU Gallery or Jakarta 32°C also play a role in sharing knowledge and know-how.**

2.3.2 Working within

Working from the perspective of what is already there, with all of its specific characteristics and actors.

2.3.2.1 Definition

We are always somewhere, at some specific location. Ruangrupa works from the perspective of what is already going on at that location, how the space is already being used, rather than what they ideally might like to project or impose upon it (as architects tend to do, consider for example Le Corbusier's Ville Radieuse, or more recently Rem Koolhaas' railway station Lille Europe). Urban planners in Western Europe often think from the drawing table and forget to work from the actual location.[22] Ruangrupa prefers to read the environment, and sees it as a starting point from which to work.

2.3.2.2 Context

Artists are expected to be able to research, to read the situation, to understand the context and to make practical use of all this knowledge. This requires the ability to observe as a researcher. In the case of ruangrupa this also means that one is part of the situation, or at least that one is related to the situation. It's not something you do for someone else, or a work commission that doesn't really have anything to do with you; rather you are always active as an equal partner.

---

[21] After more than 15 years, a new generation is gradually taking over the daily operations of the house, and assuming the responsibility of managing various new platforms.

[22] For example, the city square where I live in Rotterdam was recently redeveloped so that it could be used for outdoor events and as a place for children to play. The final design was a large bare asphalt area surrounded by a broad elevated sidewalk. The asphalt is encrusted with shiny gravel so that playing children regularly scrape their knees and elbows; the transition between the sidewalk and the central area is dangerously high and not easy to see; and anyone in a wheelchair will be altogether unable to access most of the square.

2.3.2.3 Examples

Example 1:
Vertical Villages: Ruangrupa's ArtLab and Keg De Sousa, an Australian artist, explored how temporary migrants (in this case students) organise themselves in the urban environment of Sydney. With Vertical Villages, ArtLab highlights invisible narratives/fictions in the city by casting a light on informal networks.[23]

An obvious contrast to this perspective is the skyscraper 'De Rotterdam', again by the internationally celebrated architect Rem Koolhaas. This 'vertical city' is in a number of crucial respects the exact opposite of a 'vertical village'. Though the building is expected to fulfil all of the social functions of the city, there is no feeling of informal city life. The building's main purpose is city branding and its main asset is its (inescapable) visibility.

Example 2:
The student biennale *Jakarta 32°C* in 2012 provided insight into a number of socio-cultural communities by allowing artists to participate in workshops that involved the various communities of which they were a part; the results of these workshops were presented in a final exhibition, which ultimately helped strengthen the cultural climate in the city by highlighting the various actors and by facilitating new connections.

Example 3:
Ruangrupa's 10-year anniversary event *Decompression #10*[24] also played an important role in building and maintaining ruangrupa's network. Here it was important to demonstrate the viability and the significant presence of a social movement other than the usual political and religious movements in Indonesia. The programme consisted of exhibitions, lectures, film screenings, workshops, discussions, performances, etc. showcasing ruangrupa's extensive national and international network, its variety of activities and its growth throughout the years, as well as its ability to mobilise a significant number of people.

- **'Working within' means that ruangrupa works with that which is already present. This requires the ability to recognise what is going on within the given context. 'Working within' is a method for learning to read and understand the context. This requires various skills including research skills. One must be able to read the city, to talk to people, etc.**
- **Ruangrupa showcases the inventiveness of others rather than merely appropriating it as a 'source of inspiration'.**

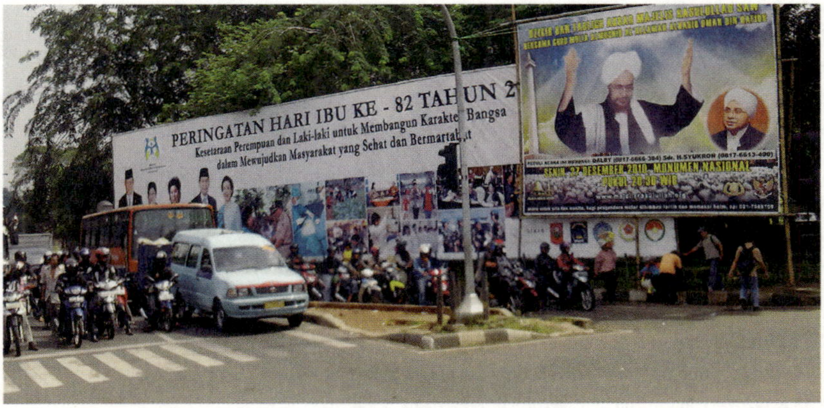

[23] For more information on the Vertical Villages project, see: *http://www.4a.com.au/vertical-villages/* and *https://www.youtube.com/watch?v=48WFAByn lAk*

[24] Ruangrupa, 'Decompression #10', programme booklet, 2010.

EXHIBITIONS ▾ EVENTS ▾ SHOP ABOUT ▾ NEWS ▾ SUPPORT ▾ RESOURCES ▾

VERTICAL VILLAGES

RUANGRUPA & KEG DE SOUZA
6 SEPTEMBER – 26 OCTOBER 2013

Home » 2013 » Exhibitions » Vertical Villages

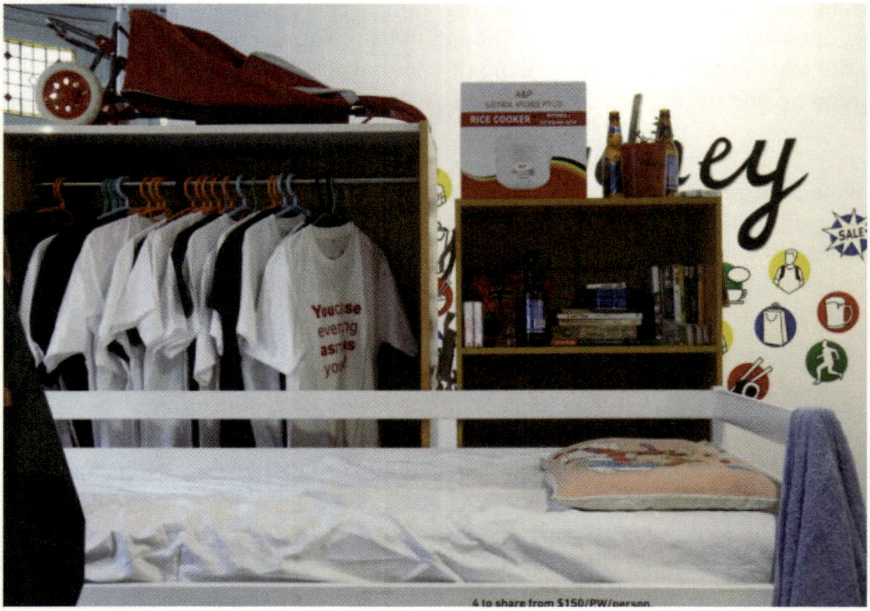

BACK NEXT

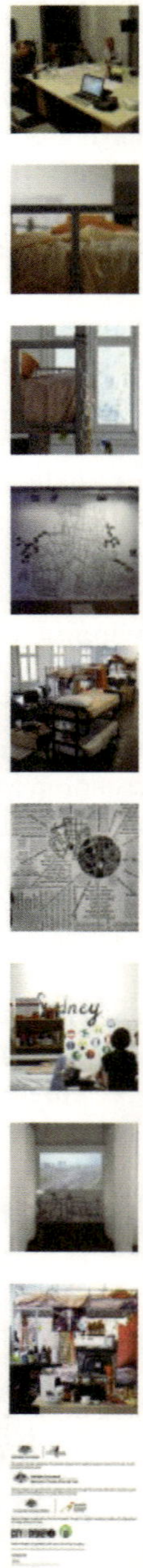

Vertical Villages is a collaborative partnership between ruangrupa ArtLab (Indonesia), Keg de Souza (Australia) and 4A Centre for Contemporary Asian Art (Australia) working with the international student population living in Sydney's CBD. Throughout July the artists' were based in 4A's ground floor gallery, utilising the street-front space as an opportunity to meet and collaborate with international students.

Vertical Villages articulates how international students engage with urban design and architecture through an amassing of personal experiences and belonging. Through a series of alternative mapping processes, Vertical Villages unpacks the individuals movements both within the city, and more broadly in the region. Personal objects and communication have also been incorporated into the exhibition as a means of highlighting the many voices of international students who participated in the project.

After intensive research, ruangrupa ArtLab and Keg de Souza recognised these students – specifically those living in high-density and multiple occupancy housing – as a group with varied understandings and expressions of domestic and communal spaces. As temporary migrants, this group illustrate the capacity of self-organisation in an unfamiliar situation, whether that may be through improvised and makeshift living situations, or a specific engagement with the urban context.

With over 35,000 international students enrolled in Sydney tertiary institutions annually, international students play an important role in the social and economic dynamic of Sydney, yet their presence within a wider conversation about the cultural and architectural development of the city.

Equally, the structure of residential living in Sydney is about to change dramatically. Developments such as World Tower, Central Park and Green Square are evidence of a shift from low to medium and high-density housing. But is the city of Sydney itself equipped for such a dramatic shift in the scale of personal and public space?

CURRENT

COMING SOON

2.3.3 Narratives and fictions in the city

Fiction, a reality born from a context.

> *'Art offers other scenarios, other fictions, it's another kind of activism... It is about writing histories next to official histories.'*
> *Ade Darmawan, 7th Freedom Lecture, October 23, 2014, organised by the political and cultural centre De Balie (Amsterdam) in collaboration with Amnesty International.* [25]

One of the central elements in the work of ruangrupa is seeking out alternative narratives and fictions, specifically in the urban environment which is a perfect situation for working with collective memory and popular culture.

2.3.3.1 Collective memory

Ruangrupa is fascinated by the realities of the 'lower' socio-economic class, and sincerely identifies with the mentality of this class, particularly its inventiveness and solutions. This is a domain of precarious relationships, self-organisation and ingenuity. Ruangrupa finds in this environment the examples and solutions for drawing attention to various issues (see for example urban printing[26]).

Fiction is applied in two different ways. First, as a strategy for sparking the imagination. Not fiction for fiction's sake, but in order to give a face to the intrinsic power of people or of a community.

Second, fiction equals invisible realities. ArtLab is the platform within ruangrupa that researches fiction in the city, brings fiction to light and thus feeds or stimulates other ruangrupa activities (see for example the project 'Vertical Villages', section 2.3.2.3, example 1). By documenting existing fictions, ArtLab and other initiatives within ruangrupa help record a collective memory of the city.

Without this awareness, part of the creative history/fiction of the city would be lost, and the dominant history/fiction would become even more dominant. In other words: the dominant position of the mainstream[27] becomes even further reinforced. Other institutes such as the Institut Sejarah Sosial Indonesia (Institute for Social History of Indonesia) also recognise the importance of cataloguing these also-narratives/fictions; members of the Institut Sejarah Sosial Indonesia stated, during a lecture in the context of the event Decompression #10 (see section 2.3.2.3, example 3) that social history is also by definition political history (who is in power?). In Indonesia as well as elsewhere, it is important to make visible and to archive other also-valid narratives.

For a broader perspective on the use of fiction as an (activist) artistic style attribute, an example worth considering here is the genre of feminist science-fiction, in which writers use the medium of science-fiction in order to present a valid also-reality.[28]

An enlightening description of the relation between fiction and reality was provided by the Spanish collective Enmedio, which sees itself as a collective 'In the midst of art, social

---

25 A video of the lecture can be seen on De Balie's Vimeo page: *https://vimeo.com/109858418*

26 Urban printing: graffiti, stickers, T-shirts, posters, etc.

27 '*The mainstream has arguably become the modern voice of a modern form of imperialism. If so, it must surely amount to one of the most effective and devastating voices that that particular form of domination has employed. Because it infiltrates almost every area of our banal lives. And because it passes almost undetected. The former is possible, because there is not a medium that the mainstream doesn't have at its disposal. As for the latter, this is possible because the mainstream's preferred semantics are those of our own largely (albeit, purely cosmetic) "progressive" values. For, just like the world of marketing that is its natural model and ally, it has learnt that for us to believe in and buy into its message, it has to represent back to us our own values (however shallow).*' Adam Warren, 'The Mainstream as Domination', in: *Counterpunch Weekend Edition*, February 6-8, 2015.

28 See for example Margaret Atwood, or the website *http://feministsf.org/*

activism, in the midst of the media':

LEO: 'It's not as we have fiction on one side, and reality on the other: fiction is the very core of reality. Everything from a demonstration (theatrical action on the streets) to the writing of a political speech (drawing on images and the imaginary), all of it is fiction. What matters are the effects of the fictions, whether or not we are able to re-appropriate them, whether or not we believe them, whether they make us feel empowered or impotent. The basis for social change is cultural: the stories that give meaning to our lives and to the world we live in.'

MARIO: 'This is why we work along two lines. On one hand, we disrupt the dominant narrative – the official explanation of the world – by means of guerrilla communication tactics: posters, slogans, messages, and so on. And on the other, we contribute to the autonomous production of imaginaries. Not by dismantling existing narratives, but by creating alternative ones. This is the most important and most difficult task: self-representation, creating our own story, our own explanation of what is happening. A narrative that we can live in.' [29]

2.3.3.2 Popular visual culture

Ruangrupa's projects are often directly related to popular visual culture. For ruangrupa this is perhaps the most important strategy for generating critical mass. It serves as a starting point to engage in conversation with each other. The critical mass is found among ruangrupa's specific public, young people and citizens of Jakarta in general. It is not easy to maintain one's credibility in such an environment, and it is to ruangrupa's credit that they have managed to do so. Obviously, popular visual culture is also co-opted by commercial ventures such as cigarette and fashion brands or manufacturers of consumer electronics, who occasionally offer to sponsor ruangrupa's projects. How to resist the temptation, in a situation without public funding or other financial support, to accept such offers from potential sponsors? And how to hold on to your own vision in choosing who and who not to collaborate with? It's a huge challenge for ruangrupa to make sure that its base camp, everything that happens in and around the house, does not gradually turn into just another meeting place for hipsters, mainstream culture, uncritical and uninteresting energy. Ruangrupa has always in a sense been a popular hangout spot. One may wonder whether an event such as Jakarta 32°C is in fact more of a lifestyle event than a critical platform. This is on one hand a point of concern, though ruangrupa also shows us that there is more than one way to consider a platform or an organisational structure. Jakarta 32°C is not only an event, it works simultaneously on a variety of levels and serves more than one goal: for example in connecting various actors (individuals and collectives) within the city, but also as a breeding ground for new initiatives, and for recruiting new members.

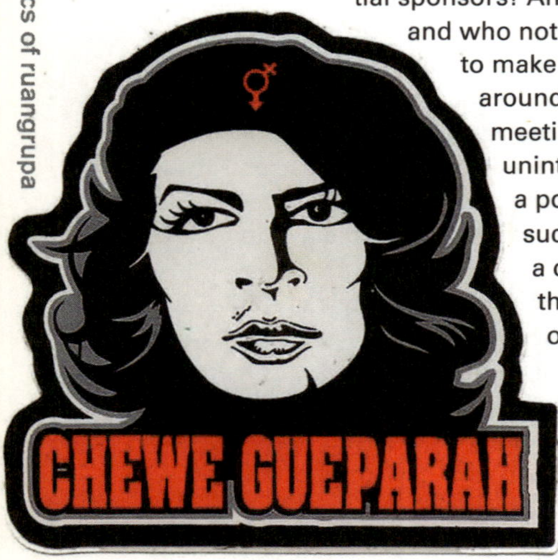

2.3.4 The collective and the individual

In section 2.2.3, 'Some basic characteristics of ruangrupa', I discussed the position of the individual within the collective, and the problem of dealing with conflicts. The question is how the individual functions within these structures.

[29] Leonedis Martin, 'Disrupt the dominant narrative', in: *SLUM Lab 8: The Social Design Public Action Reader*, Fall 2013.

2.3.4.1 Individual space

In order to work productively within a collaborative effort, an individual requires individual stimuli, an individual will. It's important that everyone should have their own projects, that individual members do not dissolve entirely within the collective. Members are stimulated to manifest themselves as individual artists (such as Julia Sarisetiati who leads RURU Corps[30]). A combination of collaborative and individual activities benefit the individual as well as the collective (see on the following page an excerpt from an online chat on this subject with Tintin Wulia).

2.3.4.2 Tasks and conflicts

How to strengthen and benefit the individual members – all members have their own idiosyncrasies, their own tasks and responsibilities, and it is up to each individual to find out how to perform and develop these tasks; everyone is free to find their own way of doing things. There is no formally defined way of how tasks should be executed or how agreements should be reached.

This doesn't make things any easier; results are not always what you may have hoped they would be, some people do things in a way that others don't necessarily appreciate. But in the end what counts is the long-term production. There will always be some degree of dissatisfaction, misunderstandings, conflicts. Learning to deal with these is simply part of the deal. This isn't always obvious however, particularly for those who aren't core members of the organisation. Members who have been around longer naturally tend to have more authority, and some personalities tend to be more respected than others.

2.3.4.3 Distributed leadership

Each member of the collective has their own area of expertise, their own points of interest within a shared direction. Since each member is working from the perspective of their own expertise, for each project there are different people who are more or less in charge, or more or less influential within the project. Also, each member has a specific role in the different departments or platforms within ruangrupa. This has two advantages: distribution of leadership, and a way of dealing with conflicts that may arise (though there may also on some level be a tendency to avoid conflicts that on another level may well be necessary or fruitful).

Each member agrees to assume a number of tasks that are more or less suitable to their particular set of competences and abilities. But no matter the nature of these tasks, all members, from the cleaning crew to the director, are always considered to be an essential element of the programmatic content. This is very different from the approach of a typical Western art institute such as De Appel in Amsterdam, where the director sets out the course and determines the programme, and the staff helps to realise this decision. What would it mean if everyone, from the director to the attendants, the building crew and the publicity staff, contributed to the programme? What if instead of a board of directors, everyone involved in the institute would contribute to formulating the institute's mission and controlling the implementation of this mission? For ruangrupa, the relationship between the collective and the individual is almost diametrically opposite to the way it is in the Western model. The ultimate responsibility always lies with the collective, an arrangement which in effect provides the individual with more challenges and more freedom. The individual is nourished by the collective but must also be able to nourish this same collective; individual development is essential in this respect.

30 Julia Sarisetiati is the manager of RURU Corps, ruangrupa's visual communication and PR department, but she was also invited to participate in the 2013 Jakarta Biennale as well as residency programmes abroad, such as Sapporo Artist in Residence (2014) or Seoul Art Space Geumcheon (2011).

a
Tintin Wulia: i actually just browsed through Claire Bishop's new book today, Artificial Hells, do you know this book?

Mas Art: yes you already mentioned it before but the guys in Beijing disapproved the book because she can not say something valid in the asian context or she does not want to try

Tintin Wulia: as i was browsing through I thought, hmm thinking of Indonesia's art scene then it sounds like it's a socialist country [...] well, indonesia is unique anyway - the government is demokrasi pancasila or whatever – the people are socialist. or anarchist. depending who you see hahahaha – the government runs itself for the sake of getting money, the people manage themselves for the sake of survival [...] well she goes through cases, basically, and the cases are only from the west or eastern west (eastern europe) – so no, she deliberately not touch asia at all – i think she doesn't know about asia at all

Mas Art: that is also normal nothing to blame her of course – but what is for you interesting in the book?

Tintin Wulia: well - just how she talks about participation generally – i don't anyway see the art world as west and east generally ... if i try to define my work, i'd define it as my work ... it's not west, not east, it's individual ... this is also what's interesting for me because the book talks about participation being collective and collaborative for me more and more the individuals have to be prominent – because i don't want to see individuals as only a part of a system ... – or, i can accept that an individual is a part of a system, but I believe s/he is actually stronger than the system ... especially when s/he interacts with another individual [...] This is one point in the book that I'm looking at:
'[A]dvanced art of the last decade has seen a renewed affirmation of collectivity and a denigration of the individual, who becomes synonymous with the values of Cold War liberalism and its transformation into neoliberalism, that is, the economic practice of private property rights, free markets and free trade. [...] Even if a work of art is not directly participatory, references to community, collectivity (be this lost or actualised) and revolution are sufficient to indicate a critical distance towards the neoliberal new world order. Individualism, by contrast, is viewed with suspicion, not least because the commercial art system and museum programming continue to revolve around lucrative single figures.' (Claire Bishop, Artificial Hells: Participatory Art and the Politics of Spectatorship, Verso, 2012, p. 12.)

Excerpts from an online chat between the Indonesian artist Tintin Wulia and myself, December 2013.

• • •

b *'The respect of the invisibility of the other, this hospitality given to the other as other not only in one's own country, in one's own home but also in oneself – in one's own body, and one's own breath, one's own mind or soul –, corresponds, for me, to a human becoming, a human being. It is not possible to reduce such a gesture to a moral imperative, it requires an availability of energy which allows us to realize it without ruining ourselves. And if, in my book I Love to You, I explain that, to recognize the other as other, I must use negativity with respect to myself – and in another way to the other –, to this new dialectical process I have to add a cultivation of energy that the Western tradition lacks.'*
Luce Irigaray, 'Being Two, How Many Eyes Have We?', in: *Paragraph*, Vol. 25, Issue 3, Jan. 2008 (text originally written in 2000), pp. 143-151.

• • •

c *'Writing on the notion of anarchy as the antipode of fascism and the fascist conception that "in unity there is strength – in uniformity there is strength," Alan Moore (2007) stresses that anarchy is almost starting from the principle that "in diversity, there is strength." Everybody is recognized as having their own abilities, agendas, and their own need to work cooperatively with other people in mutual and collaborative approaches. This is in direct contrast to the current neoliberal, capitalist, and modernist narrative that individuals are independent, without the need of community or group support. Anarchist theory foregrounds diversity as the great social reservoir of human particularity, with people, all different, working together in common towards mutual goals.'*
Liat Ben-Moshe, Dave Hill, Anthony J. Nocella II, and Bill Templer, 'Disabling Capitalism and an Anarchism of "Radical Equality" in Resistance to Ideologies of Normalcy', in: Amster et al. (eds.), *Contemporary Anarchist Studies: An Introductory Anthology of Anarchy in the Academy*, Routledge, 2009, p.113.

• • •

d *'It took me I guess two years to have the courage to say my opinion on what KUNCI is, and have my own voice about what KUNCI is doing. It's not because there is often occasions for that, but it's also the courage or knowledge of information that*

I received by being here a lot. That kind of awareness that is transmitted not in a very formal way or like a class about KUNCI history, but instead by making a coffee together or sitting here and talking about what KUNCI is, or even guests coming here and asking about KUNCI, and I keep thinking "Oh so that is KUNCI".'
Syafiatudina, quoted in: 'Toilet Tissue and Other Formless Organisational Matters', excerpt from a conversation between Antariksa (KUNCI, Yogyakarta), Binna Choi (Casco, Utrecht), Syafiatudina (KUNCI), Emily Pethick (The Showroom, London), and Ferdiansyah Thajib (KUNCI), January 31, 2015, KUNCI Cultural Studies Center, Yogyakarta, transcription by Edwinna Brennan. *http://openengagement.info/tag/the-showroom/*

• • •

'Regardless of what individuals' ideas about decision making, leadership and representation might be, and the practices that they derive from these, their general and most constant framework of interaction is best described, from the point of view of the system, as distributed leadership. It is not that there are no "leaders"; there are several, of different kinds, at different scales and on different layers, at any given time; and in principle anyone can occupy this position. That is, they are not leaderless but, if the poor wordplay can be forgiven, leaderful.'
Rodrigo Nunes, *Organisation of the Organisationless: Collective Action After Networks*, Mute/PML Books, 2014, p. 33.

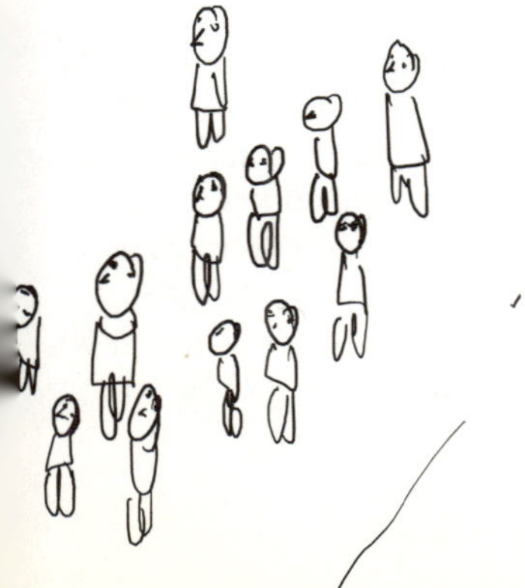

2.3.5 Shifting roles in the artistic process

2.3.5.1 Relationship with the public, the visitor, the user

The relationship between the maker and the public is no longer what it used to be. As we saw during the student biennale Jakarta 32°C (see section 2.3.2.3, example 2), the position of the maker is much more complex than simply that of a person realising an artwork – the maker is also the public, as well as the subject of the artworks. It is important to consider this relationship in terms of how we participate in society, against the background of ongoing discussions on this subject; see for example Jacques Rancière's *The Emancipated Spectator*[31] and Stephen Wright's *Toward a Lexicon of Usership.*[32] For example, how do we deal with all the chaos/noise that the corporate production machine constantly needs to generate simply to keep itself going? We could force ourselves to take a somewhat more proactive position, together with the public – so that the division between public and maker becomes more ambiguous, so that people in the public don't feel treated like ignorant customers, which people in fact never are.

2.3.5.2 Position of method/technique/product

We can conclude from the activities deployed by ruangrupa that the position of concepts such as technique, method and product has also changed. An exhibition can be applied as an educational method, a workshop can be the artwork itself. Video is seen as a social medium rather than merely a technical instrument. An NGO is used to generate an audience (see chapter 3, section 3.3.3, 'Practitioners', artist Moelyono) rather than merely as a source of income. An art installation involving the making and serving of homemade cider becomes (quite logically) a communication tool and conversation starter rather than a purely artistic endeavour (see chapter 3, section 3.3.1, 'Practitioners', collective Lifepatch). Or, to take an

---

[31] *'In his book Le spectateur émancipé Jacques Rancière reveals how the idea that in our consumer culture audiences are bound to passively absorb art and culture, has led contemporary artists and theatre makers to a variety of attempts to activate their audiences. The spectator would thus become an "emancipated" member of the cultural community. However, in the book Rancière brilliantly analyses this thesis and offers a radically different perspective on authorship.'* De Balie, 'An evening with Jacques Rancière, Mårten Spångberg and Steven ten Thije', promotional website text, March 2015. *https://vimeo.com/123248562*

[32] *'A lexicon of terms has been written by theorist Stephen Wright for the Museum of Arte Útil and can serve as a textual tool kit. The lexicon includes terms that Wright feels should be "retired" alongside what he refers to as "emergent concepts" and "modes of usership".'* Arte Útil, 'Stephen Wright: Toward a Lexicon of Usership', introductory text. *http://www.arte-util.org/tools/lexicon/*

example from the Netherlands: who exactly is the 'public' for an artist such as Jeanne van Heeswijk, whose artistic practice is an organisation (Freehouse) that promotes social cohesion by making physical, social and organisational space available for local projects, most of which have little or nothing to do with 'art' in a traditional sense?[33]

It is crucial to realise the implications of all these changes in order to be able to properly interpret the artworks and to understand where they take place, and who the intended audience or participants are. The authority of artworks takes on a different meaning, while the position of audience, maker and organiser becomes less clearly defined. This requires a different way of understanding skills, another definition of what we see as results. Personally I like to think of an artwork as a 'moment': a temporary clustering or documentation of insights and experiences which can take the form of a meeting, a sculpture, a text, a doodle, a performance, etc.

Members of ruangrupa, like all artists, need to develop and deploy such skills in order to progress from research to material production. They see themselves, as previously described in the final paragraph of chapter 1, as players of 'total football': a fluid system in which anyone can assume anyone else's position. However, one notable exception would be the goalkeeper, who in this context would have been Om Lorry, ruangrupa's bookkeeper from 2004 to 2014. And, since approximately 2010, ruangrupa's organisational structure has further grown to the point where the total football team now requires a (semi-)professional manager: Ajeng Nurul Aini.

2.3.5.3 The professional

For ruangrupa, the concept of professionalism is not about end products, time management, efficiency or a streamlined organisational structure; rather, the focus is on long-term commitment and programmatic vision, sustainability of processes, the ability to ideologically and practically connect oneself to the activities one is involved in, and to deal with the everyday consequences of these connections and activities. The practical implementation of ongoing projects is not the primary focus, and it's important to allow oneself to have a 'bad hair day' every now and then, and even to realise that this can in fact be an important part of the research, development and production process.

- **Ruangrupa shows us that there are other ways of understanding and other ways of acting. For example, the purpose of an artwork can be simply to establish a contact with the public, and thus becomes more of a facilitary tool than an end in itself; perhaps in this case a documentation of this contact will end up being the actual artwork.**
- **The public should be involved more closely with the artwork, rather than as a mere spectator, which is usually the case with 'modern' art. Artists should also see themselves as something more than an isolated avant-garde.**
- **Professionalism is not by definition product-oriented.**

2.4 A critique of ruangrupa's functioning

First of all, ruangrupa simply does too much. It's impossible for anyone to keep track of all the works being produced, which places a great deal of stress on collaborative efforts, on the various platforms, on the administrative structure of the organisation. In a modern society, in which the overproduction of goods as well as the 'production' of visibility are seen as essential requirements (otherwise one loses market value and thus political and/or economic power), an organisation such as ruangrupa is under constant pressure to go on producing, either out of necessity or simply out of habit, because people are used to doing things in a certain way and are unable to make hard choices. Ruangrupa has so many projects going on, simply because there are so many good opportunities presenting themselves and it's very

[33] For an informative video on Jeanne van Heeswijk and Freehouse, see: *http://www.arttube.nl/en/video/Boijmans/Jeanne_van_Heeswijk*

hard to turn any of these down. As the number of staff members continues to increase, there is also an increased confidence in the ability to successfully take on all these challenges, which only results in more projects and more workload.

Another factor is the personal tendency to work hard and do a lot, a strong work ethic which seems to be an essential characteristic of all core members of ruangrupa. Hafiz Rancajale, Ade Darmawan, Oomleo, Indra Ameng and others are always coming up with new plans, always busy with something else than what they were originally busy with. On one level this work ethic has to do with an identification with hard-working people; to paraphrase Ade Darmawan: let us work according to the idea of 'work'; only then can we feel we have the authority to 'say' things, with an equal voice.

Obviously an urban environment such as Jakarta also exerts a powerful influence on the competitive aspects of human nature. The struggle for visual attention such as advertisements (from small messages to the banners and billboards announcing new shopping malls under construction) is impossible to ignore, as is the daily struggle of traffic jams, poor infrastructure, street market activity, competition between street food vendors and motorcycle taxis, etc. – to say nothing of the multitude of religious groups all competing for attention. The city is a daily struggle, a daily reality check. Every possible cliché about the 'attention economy' is much more radically present in the Indonesian context than it is in a country such as the Netherlands.

Another aspect of 'doing too much' is that it is not enough to simply make a lot of unarticulated noise (or as I like to say, 'performing being a rebel') but that there is a need to be active on a practical level, to relate practically to the various contexts in which we find ourselves.

In more general terms we could say that in any modern society there is a constant pressure to attract attention, leaving little space for also-ideas, also-proposals, also-ways of acting, for providing perspectives on an also-possible world. In this sense, the need to promote your content and your agenda is an integral and inevitable part of any artistic practice. This is a very real dilemma that we observe again and again in various social and/or cultural organisations. Should we compete with mainstream culture, and if yes, then how? Ruangrupa's programme provides some answers to these questions, at least to some extent. How should an artist resist or ignore these pressures, without being seen as lazy or passive? Another option is simply to be what we are and to do what we do, without succumbing to this pressure to prove ourselves, and just carry on with our own agenda, without feeling the need to constantly justify ourselves or to advertise our opposition to whatever it is we are opposed to, but quite simply to be present in a clear and powerful way.

2.4.1 The necessity of doing too much

2.4.1.1 Doing too much: claiming territory

Due to the lack or even absence of a supporting structure, ruangrupa feels the need to act, to organise, and not only to provide a space but more importantly to create an infrastructure, in order to generate critical mass, to connect with and support kindred spirits, to learn and to exchange, to register and generate fictions in order to link one's own insights to related activities, to make alternative forces visible. This provides an opportunity to apply our ideas in a more useful way. Also, ruangrupa currently finds itself in a phase of operating increasingly on an institutional level, of being in a position to negotiate on a political level. This transition costs a great deal of time and energy, and is not without some serious learning obstacles. Sometime around 2005 ruangrupa survived a serious internal financial crisis; ten years later, let us hope that ruangrupa also manages to pull through this organisational crisis. The organisation is in a state of transition, there are many new people, the individual career of several members is flourishing; there is more than enough work to be done.

- **True involvement requires devotion, even surrender. After all, we are claiming a space that cannot then be occupied by anyone else. The question is of course whether this devotion is only about yourself, or whether you are able to apply it for the benefit of the community. Sometimes there is an opportunity or necessity to assume leadership within a 'way of being'.**

2.4.1.2 Doing too much: overdoing

Overdoing leads to an unnecessary waste of energy. Ruangrupa often seems to do things out of habit and to get involved in too many directions at once. For example, in 2014 I supervised students of the Willem de Kooning Academy participating in the Jakarta 32°C student biennale. One thing that was particularly interesting about this specific biennale was the fact that all the work presented was realised on location in the context of workshops. The idea was to research aspects of the city through a focus on one specific medium. However the biennale was not entirely successful due to a number of factors:

1. Though it was a good idea that the workshops should be led by ruangrupa members or related organisations, in practice everyone had too little time in their agendas to fully concentrate on the projects.

2a. Since ruangrupa's financial situation is still far from stable, the work budget was not clearly defined and went on being adjusted and readjusted even as the workshop was going on. This lack of clarity had a number of unpleasant consequences, for example on the production of the catalogue and the location of the final exhibition, which was changed several times during the six weeks' duration of the workshops and exhibition.

2b. Since ruangrupa initiates so many projects and ends up doing or having to do too much, there is often a great deal of organisational stress, which again makes financial matters unpredictable to say the least.

3. The manager of the biennale was simultaneously responsible for several other essential tasks, making it impossible for this single person to focus properly on making the Jakarta 32°C biennale a success.

In the meantime, ruangrupa's network of organisations and individuals with which it collaborates or plans on collaborating just keeps on growing. It is becoming increasingly difficult to have a clear overview of the programmatic and practical agenda, or even to address this situation due to a number of internal tensions or unspoken habits. In early 2015 there was an attempt to thoroughly reorganise the staff and re-evaluate the capacities. This was (and remains) necessary, since there is a real and ongoing danger that ruangrupa could become just another project factory and lose contact with its original values and objectives – which are precisely what has made ruangrupa such an interesting model for the Southeast Asian and international art world in the first place.

- **Also-valid ideas: activists or actors in the art arena should be aware not to isolate themselves in alternative or dissident strategies; the insights they generate can be valid and practical, as good or as bad as any others including those of the mainstream; in this sense there is no such thing as the monolithic inevitability of the mainstream as we understand it.**
- **How do activists or actors in the art arena operate on an institutional level? At one point we have gained a certain amount of experience, built up a network of useful connections. Tapping into this energy and these ideas on an institutional level.**
- **Bringing together kindred spirits and building infrastructures: official recognition brings with it a mentor function towards the community, towards younger like-minded individuals and groups.**

2.4.2 Other points of concern

The specific Indonesian context brings with it a certain number of pitfalls on the subject of authority. Since hierarchy and age play an important role in Indonesian culture, older and more experienced members encounter little resistance (let alone direct criticism) from younger members or partners. Also there is a natural tendency for leading voices within an institute to emphasise their own agenda above that of others. This makes it hard for them to receive constructive criticism or casual feedback on the functioning and the position of the collective. This is particularly problematic because criticism from (respected) outsiders is usually less effective and relevant than internal feedback, which often opens up new possibilities and offers new practical solutions.

2.4.2.1 Seeing oneself as the focal point

More than once I found myself asking ruangrupa members: 'Don't you think the work of members is presented a bit too often in exhibitions as a strategy for profiling these individual members as well as the collective? This actually makes your position more tenuous, and the selection of work sometimes feels a bit forced.' An example was the exhibition 'Face-Dominated' during the festival OK. Video FLESH 2011, in which curator Hafiz Rancajale (a ruangrupa member) planted a number of more or less subtle statements, related to the fact that members of ruangrupa felt they were not taken entirely seriously and did not receive the credit they deserved within the official Indonesian art world. Ruangrupa has played and still plays an important role in cultivating young artists and curators and thus in developing an artistic language; having invested so much, many of its members felt that they did not receive the attention and recognition they deserved, that there is not enough exchange going on, that artists are being shielded, that curators are too busy protecting their own agendas. The most important criticism is that the art world is not giving back enough to the community.[34]

However, my feedback on this issue and on (for example) this particular exhibition was mostly dismissed by ruangrupa members. If others do not give them the credit they are due, then they feel it is up to them to claim this credit, for example by adding an extra exhibition programme to the 2011 OK. Video festival in commercial galleries. It's a perfectly understandable reaction – though I must admit that I myself tend to be less proactive in such situations.

Although ruangrupa regularly involves partners from the more 'formal' art scene in their activities, these partners seldom return the favour. This means that the exchange of knowledge becomes a one-way transaction, and that ruangrupa is not organically visible in these other contexts. Ruangrupa regularly seeks contact with (and gives space and visibility to) artists and curators whom they don't yet know so well, and involves them in its programme. One possible reason why things sometimes go wrong (or turn out different than expected) and why there is a lack of reciprocity, is due to a degree of inefficiency in communication and/or cooperation, as well as the unconcentrated way in which things are sometimes done.

2.4.2.2 Working with or within

Though being part of the local community is a crucial dimension for ruangrupa, the collective is not really rooted in the actual neighbourhood where the house is located.

The location of the house was mostly determined by the need to be easily accessible and near the city centre, and yet in a residential neighbourhood rather than an office district. In a sense this is not really a problem since ruangrupa is deeply rooted in the city as a whole; connecting with the neighbourhood would however provide opportunities for projects founded on an even more horizontal approach based on social relationships. Currently, projects tend to develop from cultural relationships; 'nongkrong' takes place mostly with artists and cultural activists from outside the neighbourhood. Farid Rakun, ruangrupa

34 A similar discontent or impatience can be observed in many organisers and/or artists and is on more than one level perfectly understandable.

member since 2010 (and loosely involved since 2003) suggested I take a look in this context at the work of the American 'social practice' installation artist Theaster Gates at the 2012 Documenta, though it wasn't clear to me why exactly (and I still haven't figured it out).

2.4.2.3 The (official?) art world

Perhaps ruangrupa would benefit by being more bold in distancing itself from the official art world, rather than trying on some level to connect or remain connected to it. One may wonder whether it is worth all the energy required to prove oneself within this world. On the other hand, there is no denying that such contacts also provide a number of important tools and resources.

Ruangrupa already has a fully-fledged and influential programme of its own, and several of its members hold positions in government committees. Ruangrupa succeeded in redefining the Jakarta Biennale, and thereby also more generally revitalising what a biennale's function can be. It seems to me that ruangrupa too often wants to teach others a lesson, or perhaps I simply don't understand the finer points of what motivates ruangrupa, in my opinion, to spend too much time and energy proving itself. One possible explanation for the need to be involved on so many different levels is the fact that there are almost no official art institutes or independent museums in Indonesia (which may actually be a good thing). There are on one hand artists' initiatives, and on the other hand the mainstream art market of private initiatives and collectors, and not much breathing space in between. In the Netherlands on the other hand, and despite the succession of economic, political and cultural crises, there are still enough paths for artists to move up and down and back up again through the various art spaces, from Upominki to W139 and De Fabriek, and from SMBA to De Vleeshal and back to Vous Etes Ici, then to De Service Garage, next from Het Wilde Weten in Rotterdam to an apartment exhibition in Antwerp, to finally present your book at Onomatopee in collaboration with Casco. In other words, an artist in the Netherlands has a variety of levels on which to operate. In Indonesia this is much more limited, which makes a significant difference.

2.4.2.4 Conflict management

Javanese tradition dictates that one should never be too explicit or straightforward. Addressing doubts or criticism is therefore often complicated and requires time. Solutions are expected to emerge from the work itself. Criticism is seen as not so relevant and is usually solved in other ways, as described earlier in this chapter, such as the concept of distributed leadership; however this doesn't solve everything. Agreements or decisions are often unclear, conflicts are postponed. For some this is a productive system, but for others it leads to frustration. However, since this is a collective endeavour, the unspoken frustrations and irritations (inherent to any community or collaborative effort) might be given more space in the house of ruangrupa.

2.4.2.5 Financial basis, sponsorship, etc.

RURU Corps, which was set up in 2011, is the department within ruangrupa responsible for finding sponsors, NGOs and commercial projects in order to finance ruangrupa's activities. RURU Corps makes use of the efforts and knowledge of ruangrupa members, though there is little in-house experience in the field of fundraising. It will be interesting to go on monitoring how RURU Corps functions and can function in the near future. Will it become a traditional management or PR department, or will it be able to apply the spirit of ruangrupa's activities in the field of fundraising? For example, will there be an effort to implement the idea of solidarity economy, or the principle of 'gotong royong'? Or will ruangrupa, despite all good intentions, ultimately become part of an opportunistic art world that prefers to work with concepts and has no time to develop organically from a context? Rather than projects that grow from commitment, from a (necessary) waste of time, from building relationships, etc.

2.4.3 And finally...

Another problem resulting from the points I have raised above is that sometimes one would wish for more peer evaluation and more reflection on one's own functioning, as exemplified by the following quotation, an excerpt from a grant application for the Singapore Biennale which I was allowed to consult:

> *'Since ruangrupa is not only a few artists that [are] gathering and working together for our individual benefit or even for just the sake of the group, [what] we're really trying to do is work at the connection between art and the Indonesian social context. And it's very important to provide a mental and physical space for artists and people to develop their ideas and carry out study, research, collaboration and project-based works. We believe that only in this way can art reach a critical point. We believe art should take its social and political surroundings into account – in our case urban problems and urban visual culture. We questioned public space, housing problems, urban printing production, city government, visual propaganda, city structure, audio visual culture, youth culture, people's survival in the city etc... All things that people in general experience, and it makes it easy for people to see and relate the work back to them. "Art people" may discuss whether or not it is art – but we don't care about that... it's always like an orgasm for us when we make them confused... hehehe.'*

This excerpt seems rather vague and unfocused to me; it makes me wonder about ruangrupa's values and direction, and more worryingly whether the development of ruangrupa may have reached its final phase. I would have expected something more specific at this point. However, another excerpt from the same text could help inspire confidence that ruangrupa still has a vision for long-term development and is still setting itself new goals which may not always be obvious to outsiders:

> *'We're thinking it's not only a protest or being reactive against the so called mainstream, commercial or whatever, this kind of mode mostly short term and short impact as well. We try to be more strategic and long term in this sense, we try to develop a different other structure. Like I mention above about trying to shift the mode of creative process, or for example when we think the art education or education in general is sucks, then we must try to develop kind of "alternative" way, giving new reference-points and alternative angles etc through our activity. As far as audiences are concerned, we never really care about arty audiences – like I mention above as well, we're more interested in making*

ruru.net at the 10th anniversery of ruangrupa

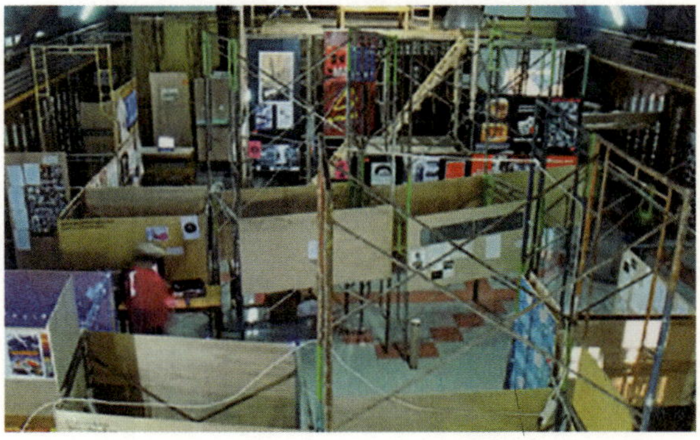

'In the last ten years, ruangrupa has observed the development of space, public and their activities that endlessly and dynamically grow with the artistic and cultural organizations. The exhibition will chronologically present the collaboration held between ruangrupa and other organizations, collectives, communities, and its professional networks, local and foreign. This outline of events tries to remap the forms of cross-disciplinary collaboration occurred through art projects, workshops, exhibitions, seminars, discussions, and artistic residencies. On the other hand, the ruru.net exhibition will also exhibit the recapitulation of the journey so far, documentation and current projects from ruangrupa's partners, which are still active to the present day, such as from Akademi Samali, ELSAM, Forum Lenteng, Grafis Sosial, Institut Sejarah Sosial Indonesia, Kineforum, PenitiPink, Sanggar Akar dan Serrum (Jakarta), Asbestos Art Space dan Commonroom (Bandung), Jatiwangi Art Factory (Jatiwangi), Gardu Unik (Cirebon), BYAR Creative Industry (Semarang), Daging Tumbuh, KUNCI Cultural Study Center dan MES56 (Yogyakarta), C.E.I.A (Brazil), Casco and Montevideo (Netherland), Gang Festival and Engagemedia (Australia), Kuratoriskaktion (Denmark), Skulpturenpark/KUNSTrePUBLIK (Germany), and Video Art Center Tokyo (Japan).' Ruangrupa, 'Decompression #10', programme booklet, 2010.

"new audiences"... because when we make something different to galleries why should we should expect the same audiences? Of course, it takes some time to develop this, but when we do it in a very clear way and with strong consistency it will be develop naturally, because it's all related and we should see audiences as a mutual and horizontal partner not as a "target market" like if you selling your cakes'.

The challenge for ruangrupa, in relation to my concerns about the lack of self-reflection and self-criticism on the functioning of the organisation, is similar to more general concerns expressed in the quotation below by the Brazilian philosopher Euclides André Mance on the subject of solidarity economy. The problems or challenges for ruangrupa are in themselves not specific to the art world, but are something that keeps popping up in many such movements, particularly movements that propose different models of political and economic participation. Mance, a founding member of the Philosophy of Liberation Institute, describes here two pitfalls typical of contemporary solidarity economy. The first is a limited understanding within progressive social forces of what solidarity economy actually implies, combined with a tendency by capitalist forces to co-opt the phenomenon by linking it to the idea of social responsibility:

'Many thus conclude that solidarity economy is simply a form of capitalism that takes social responsibility seriously. This prejudice, particularly within the left, along with certain sectors of the right, turns the burden of proof against solidarity economy, forcing it to present justifications regarding its historical possibility rather than drawing the debate to the effectiveness of its present historical reality – one where workers have become owners of self-managed enterprises and decide democratically what to do with them, collaborating with other enterprises in ways that are advantageous to all.'

The second pitfall identified by Mance is the tendency of actors in the field of solidarity economy to present themselves as 'moderate' in order to acquire funding, particularly from public sources:

' [...] solidarity economy actors looking for funding from public, particularly State bodies, tone down the antagonistic and revolutionary character of this new economy, creating room for ambiguous readings that allow them to be lumped in with social and environmental responsibility talk. Moreover, while the debate rages on about whether the values of solidarity economy will not get lost along the way, large chunks of progressive social sectors still consume non-solidarity products without questioning the effects of their consumption, which feeds back into local and global capitalist circuits.' [35]

The same problems can also be encountered in the art world, which shows how difficult it is for artists and other critical thinkers to avoid becoming entangled in those same (neo-liberal) mechanisms that they don't really want to be a part of. A substantially different setup is required, one which on one hand is equipped to deal with the dominant mode of thinking[36] and on the other hand is able to provide this substantially different setup with the necessary action radius in which to develop its own unique characteristics.

[35] Euclides André Mance, 'Solidarity Economics', Instituto de Filosofia da Libertação, 2007. *http://solidarius.com.br/mance/biblioteca/turbulence-en.pdf*

[36] The dominant way of thinking or the neoliberal system is not going to just disappear, nor is it likely to be overthrown anytime soon, regardless of whether or not this would even be desirable. For example, many artists are incapable of making ends meet without having to depend on precarious low-wage jobs focused on maximising shareholder profits.

2.5 A preliminary conclusion from the points raised so far in this chapter

I have examined a number of projects and platforms within ruangrupa, showing how ruangrupa is active and how it implements its projects. I will now try to distil from these observations a number of general characteristics, and relate these to my proposal for an individual or collective art practice which is not focused on the production of goods – an art practice which is instead based on the collection of 'notes' or 'moments', as artefacts of activities that take place as a result of actively engaging with the environments in which we live, a collection of moments to which the artist contributes individually or collectively, or which the artist simply observes.

This artistic practice, which I have called '(g)Locally Embedded Art Practice' or gLEAP, is based on the idea that artists should consider themselves as an integral part of the various communities with which they are involved, rather than as 'community builders' which is an attitude characteristic of 'community art'. The work produced and presented is not determined or generated by the community, rather it is rooted in the community. It is an element of this community rather than a final product.

We could draw a parallel with an auto mechanic living and working in the neighbourhood. The mechanic can fulfil an essential function in the cohesion of the neighbourhood by functioning as an educator, a collector of anecdotes, a person with professional knowledge and insight, a resident just like any other, etc. The mechanic's workshop can be a meeting place on a variety of levels. In this sense the mechanic's professional practice can be said to be locally embedded.[37]

In such an artistic practice, the environment in which the artist works can be seen as a 'supportive structure' (see also section 2.3.1.1), an environment focused in the first place on mutually sharing and promoting knowledge and information. However it is just as important to allow this 'supportive structure' to be or become part of a broader movement, and to link one's activities with those of other local groups or other global movements. A broader movement makes it possible to be active on micro and macro levels without getting lost in abstract or semi-contextual themes.[38] [39] It is important for artists to work within their own defined context, as well as with an eye on the broader situation. As we can see, an artistic practice is a) connected on a practical level to observed urgencies, b) connected with the chosen theme in a way that is not merely conceptual and detached, and c) part of a broader active dynamic on a (g)local level.

Ruangrupa's programme in relation to gLEAP:

Ruangrupa is built around an ongoing dialogue with the environment and with its own artistic/cultural community, in a way that does not need to adhere to any specific theme. Humour, alertness, relating to your direct environment, curiosity, your own specialisations are all healthy qualities. You relate in a focused or unfocused way to your environment, your context. This happens together with others ('nongkrong'). The projects usually originate from an existing social structure or happening and are focused on the socio-cultural environment, rather than only taking place within an 'art for art's sake' discourse.

The inner drive of each member is a basic condition for commitment as well as collaboration. As I have said before, these collaborations are consciously or unconsciously connected to a variety of communities, and focus on a variety of subjects or fields of expertise.

---

[37] An interesting example in this respect is Leeszaal Rotterdam West, a grassroots library which was set up after the neighbourhood libraries in Rotterdam (and the rest of the Netherlands) had been shut down due to budget cuts. Leeszaal Rotterdam West is based on an understanding that the social function of public libraries goes far beyond merely lending books: for example as a neutral meeting place, something crucial in a shrinking public domain. See *http://www.leeszaalrotterdamwest.nl/*

[38] Interesting in this context is an interview with Naomi Klein by Liam Barrington-Bush, 'We're not who we were told we were', in: *Contributoria: the independent journalism network*, October 2014.

[39] See also: Rodrigo Nunes, *Organisation of the Organisationless: Collective Action After Networks*, Mute/PML Books, 2014.

Being aware of each other's limitations in terms of programming or articulation also makes it possible to connect, to support each other and to visibly promote themes within a public agenda. From a personal level to a (g)locally institutional level within a socio-cultural environment. Understanding that the individual activity is part of a greater whole, and actively and patiently applying this understanding.

(What's so special about me? Anything I can think of, many other people will probably be thinking as well. So what's the relevance of seeing myself as 'alternative'?)

The idea of 'art and creativity' is often related to a kind of art that focuses on social platforms and is applied as an instrument. The combination of these words always sounds awkward, but could they also be defined in another way? On one level it's about generating empowerment and self-confidence in individuals and communities that would otherwise be overwhelmed or simply find themselves in opposition against the hegemony of a (possible) reality (read: liberal democracy), an also-reality among other realities. The element of fiction is an important method for ruangrupa to make visible also-realities, also-existences (other methods often applied are the use of poetry and noise.[40] Ruangrupa extracts fiction from its direct context, by examining the actions and customs of (groups of) people who come up with answers and solutions to smaller and larger urgencies.

However ruangrupa is also aware that fiction is not the sole domain of artists, but can be found everywhere in everyday life. This can also help us increase our awareness of the position of the public. The public does not depend on the artist; rather, it is a question of generating content together, or of making it possible for people to work with also-content (here I am paraphrasing the words of Arief Yudi, a member of Jatiwangi Art Factory, in the context of the festival for JAF's eighth anniversary[41]). Maybe the neighbour's activities are more interesting than the artist's production. One of the roles of the artist is to show that also-reality can in fact be quite natural, even obvious. This means that a gLEAP practice is part of a platform for showcasing everything that is also-present. Your own activities take place alongside those of others. Sometimes you will be the maker, sometimes the public, sometimes an assistant, etc.

2.6 Development of ruangrupa: the first 15 years

I have described the functioning of ruangrupa based on a number of its activities, and from this I have distilled a number of characteristics which are common to Indonesian collectives in general, characteristics that are specific to ruangrupa, and also characteristics that are in some way problematic. I would now like to take another approach, and that is to show how ruangrupa works with colleague artists and partners from the socio-cultural field, by describing the collective from the perspective of its chronological development. If we consider the 15 years in which ruangrupa has been active, we can distinguish four more or less clearly delineated periods.

Ruangrupa originated from a network of concert/event organisers (as art academy students) in the period between 1995 and 2000. Using a residential house as a meeting place for friends and acquaintances, the network developed into a infrastructure for nurturing and promoting socio-cultural production.

2.6.1 2000-2002 – 'Alternative space': ruangrupa as a house

Ruangrupa started as a traditional 'alternative art space'. A house, a platform for artists to stimulate and support each other's activities, to discover what it means to have a place of your own.

Such initiatives often start from a house situation: sometimes from a direct urgency to

[40] Though many noise artists reject the term 'music', they tend to present their works in the same way as musicians do (recordings, concerts). For an interesting exploration of the artistic concept of noise, see for example Mattin & Anthony Iles (eds.), *Noise & Capitalism*, Arteleku Audiolab, 2009.

[41] See chapter 3, section 3.3.2, 'Practitioners', collective Jatiwangi Art Factory. See also the Vimeo page of INDO/ART/NOW for a documentary on this festival and on Jatiwangi Art Factory: *https://vimeo.com/77838256*

come into action, sometimes from an informal, natural, contextually logical way of meeting each other.[42] Such initiatives are often by, and for, artists. For ruangrupa this was no different, and up to the present day ruangrupa has always worked from a house situation. Though it was never actually somebody's house, it was always a residential building which they rented as an artist's collective (though people can sleep and stay there, it has never been anyone's permanent residence). Ruangrupa's first house was located in the semi-gated community Komplek Garuda, once built for employees of the national airline Garuda Indonesia. This was a good starting point from which to support each other's artistic learning processes, and to build knowledge by engaging in dialogue with local and international guests. It was a hospitable place, which besides a meeting place was also a production place. Being in contact with daily life happened from a secluded space in a secluded community where the city did not directly manifest itself. Ruangrupa documented its activities through the journal Karbon.

- **The traditional 'alternative space' is characterised by using a house as a place for and by artists, a secluded location in which to develop an (engaged) practice, individually and together with colleague artists.**

2.6.2 2002-2007 – 'Also-space': building platforms, making connections with socio-cultural activities and partners in the city

(See the insert to chapter 3 for a detailed explanation of the concept of also-space.)

Ruangrupa builds platforms for production. Whether consciously or unconsciously, ruangrupa has always seen itself as a platform, even before it was properly established. Many of its members were involved in the mid-1990s as art students in Jakarta and Yogyakarta organising events and exhibitions.

Though the initial focus for ruangrupa was to build a platform for its own members, it soon became clear that in doing so ruangrupa was filling a void for a generation (as were many other comparable initiatives in those days) – a void which was the result of decades of dictatorship and censorship. For example, ruangrupa initiated a research of the use and application of the medium 'video' (which eventually led to the OK. Video festival; see also the section on OK. Video in the first insert to the present chapter).

This void also meant that there was a need to gain knowledge and experience through an international network. Ruangrupa was aware at an early stage of the phenomenon of 'networking' in order to acquire information and share knowledge. During what we could refer to as ruangrupa's second period, there was a great deal of emphasis on building platforms, which also meant finding out how to do so, what this involves, who to collaborate with, etc. These platforms served to fill voids in the cultural infrastructure of Jakarta and all of Indonesia. The platforms OK. Video and Jakarta 32°C are clear examples of this, as are more modest efforts such as the Wednesday film club (Rabu Video Club), which allowed ruangrupa to come in contact with other socio-cultural groups. The ruangrupa house was a neutral space for showing certain films and for making connections between various networks and communities.

Besides making connections between socio-cultural actors in the city (allowing them to support each other's activities and to learn from each other's vocabulary), the platforms were closely connected to what was actually going on in the city. OK. Video for example did not approach the medium of video from an art perspective, but from the given fact of the unavoidable presence and social position of the medium in the urban landscape. On one hand these platforms serve to build up and strengthen a network within the socio-cultural

[42] Several cultural initiatives in Indonesia started out in a residential house: Lifepatch, Trotoart, Jatiwangi Art Factory, KUNCI, Commonroom, MES 56, etc. Some cultural initiatives I have been personally involved in that started out in a house are: Ruimte-X, De Player, Foundation B.a.d, HomeShop.

domain, on the other hand they originate from the existing situation in the city. Ruangrupa is active with (and from) that which is already in movement, that which is already happening, and works from there. Rather than showing experimental videos, ruangrupa sets up a festival based on the existing (social) use of the medium in its local context. From the perspective of the presence of video in malls, restaurants and markets, from the pervasiveness of digital media – for example in the 'Digital Viral' programme (part of the festival OK. Video FLESH 2011) curated by Farah Wardani and described by herself as follows:

> *'Digital Viral ran an experiment to [study] patterns of video movement in the virtual realm with a participatory strategy. We invited several contributors to act as sharers as well as filterers of videos previously uploaded to the virtual realm. They recommended their video findings and will get an active reaction from 25 individuals. This sharing period went on for one month, from August to September 2011. Most of the interaction took place via Twitter. From the respondents, we received a contribution of hundreds of video links with varying themes. We then selected these videos and grouped them thematically. The themes were selected based on issues that prevail and able to represent the symptoms as well as the function of using video on the internet by Indonesians today. 26 themes were finally set: Political Spoofs, Music Spoofs, Film Spoofs, Gender, Accidents, Hoax, Idol, Talent Show: Irul Kevin, Pranks, Mainstream Celebrities, Viral Celebrities, Activism, Hacking, Science, Leaks, Moral Messages, Supernatural-Mystical, How-To, Sports, Local Genius, Experimentation, Pluralism, Religion, Lipsync, and Million Viewers.'*[43]

It was a provocative programme, focusing on the user/consumer rather than on an art audience; a programme that did not aim to convince the audience, but rather to provide us with a glimpse of our contemporary narratives, and of possible uses of the omnipresent medium of video. How do you present digital video? Where does the video take place? Who is the author? What is the carrier of the volatile medium, what is the 'status' of the digital files? How do the viewers and users relate to the medium? What are the makers trying to tell us? What are the professional skills involved? How should we read the composition of the image? Etc.

- **An important characteristic of an 'also-space' is that the programme of artists is determined by what is already happening in their environment, by seeking connections with kindred spirits in the broader socio-cultural field. It relates to the city on a practical level, rather than from the perspective of a conceptual vision.**

2.6.3 2008-2014 – 'Negotiation space': building a network and becoming an institution

> *'The principle of organization must not issue a center created in advance to capture the whole and impose itself upon it but on the contrary, it must come from all sides to create nodes of coordination, natural centers to serve all these points.'*[44]

The above quotation by the Russian anarchist Volin has a great deal in common with the position espoused and practised by ruangrupa. Ruangrupa always sees itself as part of a greater whole, rather than a focal point (though some may disagree about this). Criticism and comments on ruangrupa are welcome, and more importantly others are welcome to set up initiatives or places that take over or complement parts of the role played by ruangrupa.

For ruangrupa, building a network means knowing who is doing what, and making use of each other's experiences while being open to new input and to new ways of seeing things. By collectively generating critical mass and collective interest, the energy and

43 Source: *https://issuu.com/okvideo/docs/catalogue_flesh_2011_complete/73*

44 Volin, quoted in: Daniel Guérin, *Anarchism: From Theory to Practice.*

preoccupations of the network become more visible within the public domain. This emphasis on the necessity of organisation is an essential characteristic of ruangrupa. The OK. Video edition Militia (2007) focused on strengthening local communities and increasing social resilience. At Decompression #10, the public event related to its 10th anniversary, ruangrupa demonstrated its ability to mobilise a significant number of local young people, to call upon an extensive and impressive local and international network, and to successfully organise a relatively large event. This serves as an also-presence, a counterweight, however modest, to the usual religious, political and creative-industry events.

Ruangrupa, or at least a number of its platforms, are increasingly becoming institutions. There are two reasons for this. One is the long-term commitment of actively relating to the city and to existing networks, which has allowed ruangrupa to gain experience and knowledge and become an increasingly important player in the socio-cultural field. Increasingly, ruangrupa is also able to apply this experience on a larger scale. This means that it is becoming a serious partner and a presence that cannot be ignored alongside other cultural, social, religious or political institutions. Ruangrupa is present in the public debate and is a voice, however marginal in the larger scheme of things, that cannot be ignored. The lack of a structural cultural infrastructure in Indonesia, the evolution of ruangrupa as a cultural production centre, and its extensive long-term experience also mean on some level that it now has no choice but to operate as an institution.

For example, ruangrupa was one of six winners of the Social Enterprise Challenge for Arts, Creative & Tourism Organisations organised by DIAGEO and the British Council Indonesia, and was even asked by the British Council in Jakarta to give workshops on organisation and management. On the other hand, ruangrupa would be unlikely to pass any kind of formally organisational audit or review. On a pragmatic level however, it is rather amazing to see how much they are actually able to accomplish based on what is essentially an inefficient organisational structure. On a certain level this also shows how one-dimensional our liberal-democratic perspective on professional efficiency really is. Such a lack of 'professionalism' may also provide some kind of protection against unwanted institutionalisation and bureaucratisation, or becoming an institution where work gets done and nothing else counts anymore. In this way, ruangrupa can remain a credible player within its own network.

Ruangrupa has become a representative for a generation of artists producing and presenting their works in alternative spaces and also-spaces. Ruangrupa enjoys the support of a number of socio-cultural partners and plays a role in determining the public agenda. A number of members have a seat on the Jakarta Arts Council, one member is the chairperson of the Jakarta Biennale foundation, etc. However, with institutional recognition inevitably comes the danger (and temptation) of becoming just one more artists-for-artists community. The Indonesian art scene is enjoying an unprecedented period of international visibility. Organisations such as ruangrupa and ArtLab, as well as individual artists, are recognised and incorporated within the international art discourse. Ade Darmawan is exhibiting his works in the Porticus (Frankfurt), Reza Afisina had an exhibition in the Palais de Tokyo (Paris) and has works in the collection of the Guggenheim (New York), while the British curator Charles Esche was invited to curate the Jakarta Biennale. In addition, ruangrupa is physically expanding to the point where the house needs to be more efficiently arranged and organised (including security[45]).

For the time being, the main priority for ruangrupa is to continue building its network, rather than positioning itself as an institution; the fact of becoming an institution is seen as incidental.

Ruangrupa is also increasingly becoming a negotiation partner. Within the artistic climate of Indonesia, ruangrupa is seen as an influential representative of a specific cultural sector and plays an important role in determining the cultural climate of Jakarta, while also being closely involved in the socio-cultural field.

45 Security is handled by friends from Trotoart, another artists' organisation located in a 'rough' neighbourhood in the northern part of Jakarta.

- **In other words, a negotiation space is a position you gradually assume or grow into, in which you are a spokesperson or representative for a generation, for a network. You have the qualities necessary to bring together people and organisations, on a local, regional and international level.**

2.6.4 After 2015 – Regeneration?

In 2015-2016, ruangrupa once again finds itself at a crossroads. A younger generation is ready to play a greater role within what is now an established and proven entity. Is ruangrupa starting all over again?

Whatever happens now, or however we will end up describing this period, only time will tell. One important change has already started taking place: in 2015 the organisational structure of ruangrupa was reshuffled, and a younger generation of artists and curators have taken over a number of platforms. The early members (Ade Darmawan, Indra Ameng, Hafiz Rancajale, Reza Afisina, Oomleo) have handed over daily operations in order to focus on broader long-term developments for the house in Jakarta and the internationally active artists' collective. The challenge will be to see to what extent these early members will be willing or able to make room for the younger generation; and for the younger generation, the question is to what extent they will be able to appropriate for themselves the apparently comfortable setting they have inherited, while navigating its pitfalls such as a still fragile financial foundation.

For some time now ruangrupa has risked losing grip on what an also-space is or can be. The house is gradually becoming more functionally organised, it is more difficult than before for guests to stay a few nights. The third generation of ruangrupa members or collaborators mostly go to the house only to work or to get something specific done.

2.7 Conclusion

In relation to my concept of gLEAP and how this manifests itself in the way ruangrupa operates, the phase of the also-space is the most relevant. The mentality here is a practical one; projects, no matter how small, are simply started in the knowledge that if they are relevant enough, they have the potential to grow into something more structural, or to connect to other movements in the (g)local world. And if not, the projects will probably lead to something else. Ruangrupa as an also-space is first and foremost a socially engaged or socially critical art practice that constantly evaluates and reformulates itself simply by being active.[46] Perhaps the also-space is by definition a temporary constellation, a moment in

---

[46] We should not underestimate the value of a negotiation space, in the sense that being strategically active may well be an inevitable necessity in this day and age. In this context, an interesting description of the distinction between tactic and strategy was formulated by Michel de Certeau: *'I call a "strategy" the calculus of force-relationships which becomes possible when a subject of will and power (a proprietor, an enterprise, a city, a scientific institution) can be isolated from an "environment." A strategy assumes a place that can be circumscribed as proper (propre) and thus serve as the basis for generating relations with an exterior distinct from it (competitors, adversaries, "clienteles," "targets," or "objects" of research). Political, economic, and scientific rationality has been constructed on this strategic model. I call a "tactic," on the other hand, a calculus which cannot count on a "proper" (a spatial or institutional localization), nor thus on a borderline distinguishing the other as a visible totality. The place of a tactic belongs to the other. A tactic insinuates itself into the other's place, fragmentarily, without taking it over in its entirety, without being able to keep it at a distance. It has at its disposal no base where it can capitalize on its advantages, prepare its expansions, and secure independence with respect to circumstances. The "proper" is a victory of space over time. On the contrary, because it does not have a place, a tactic depends on time-it is always on the watch for opportunities that must be seized "on the wing." Whatever it wins, it does not keep. It must constantly manipulate events in order to turn them into "opportunities." The weak must continually turn to their own ends forces alien to them. This is achieved in the propitious moments when they are able to combine heterogeneous elements (thus, in the supermarket, the housewife confronts heterogeneous and mobile data-what she has in the refrigerator, the tastes, appetites, and moods of her guests, the best buys and their possible combinations with what she already has on hand at home, etc.); the intellectual synthesis of these given elements takes the form, however, not of a discourse, but of the decision itself, the act and manner in which the opportunity is "seized."'* Michel de Certeau, *The Practice of Everyday Life*, University of California Press, 1984.

time, a process and a journey, a step in building something small into something that refers to a larger whole. Also-space also involves the necessity to regularly be 'in the moment'. Ruangrupa is never finished, it is constantly being triggered by external stimuli and is always on the way to becoming something else, and thus only coincidentally (at least up to this point) institutional.

Ruangrupa operates based on personal relationships and affinities rather than a conceptual programme. In this context, the anarchist theoretician Paul Routledge described the concept of 'affinity' as:

'Practically, affinity consists of a group of people sharing common ground and who can provide supportive, sympathetic spaces for its members to articulate, listen to one another, and share concerns, emotions, or fears.'

For Routledge, the principle of affinity is based on solidarity, consensus-based decision-making and collaboration:

'The politics of affinity enables people to provide support and solidarity for one another. Ideally, such a politics of research should be built on consensus-decision making which is non-hierarchical and participatory-embodying flexible, fluid modes of action. The common values and beliefs articulated within the politics of affinity constitute a "structure of feeling" resting upon collective experiences and interpretations, which are cooperative rather than competitive, and which are predicated upon taking political action.' [47]

This definition, linked to consciously incorporating your whole environment (rather than only your art-related contacts) in your programme, provides an also-space with a solid foundation for being once in a while 'in the moment'.

Based on my research of ruangrupa, I will now explore a number of findings as a first step in revitalising a (contemporary) artistic practice, or in other words moving 'from hot to something else', as described in chapter 1.

2.7.1 Working contextually

The connection between how artists think and how artists act in a socially engaged practice is broken, or at least dysfunctional. Projects are often (perfectly) logical on a conceptual level, but contextually there is little or no real connection. A summary of a discussion on the theme of living-room economies (initiated by Henk van Dillen, former business economist and future adventurer) begins by referring to a project during the 2012 International Architecture Biennale Rotterdam:

'The evening started with a video titled WIJKonomie Tarwewijk ("Weconomy in the Tarwewijk neighbourhood") based on an initiative by the stichting DROOG. This top-down project was implemented in the Tarwewijk neighbourhood, where the designer Jan Konings and others presented a future scenario for the neighbourhood inspired on the theme of living-room economies. The questions that arose from this project provide some interesting starting points for a discussion: for example, are residents actually interested in making their living-room economies more visible? What is the advantage structurally for residents, what are the actual results of this kind of top-down initiatives? Those who set up this kind of projects often get paid, but is there any money left for the residents? Isn't that what it should be all about?' [48]

[47] Paul Routledge, 'Toward a relational ethics of struggle', in: Amster et al. (eds.), *Contemporary Anarchist Studies: An Introductory Anthology of Anarchy in the Academy*, Routledge, 2009, p. 85

[48] Stichting Zuidzijde, 'Rondetafelgesprek huiskamereconomie: Samenvatting', 2014. *http://www.stichtingzuidzijde.nl/wp-content/uploads/samenvatting_rondetafelgesprek_huiskamereconomie_v2.pdf*

There is a professional habit of thinking and working in terms of projects, but by cutting up everything into projects and arranging public funding accordingly, there is no room left to work on building sustainable long-term solutions.

Focusing on understanding what it means to be part of a community, rather than on professionalism with its specialist jargon, activities, closed networks, etc. should be an important element in a future artistic practice. The problem for art education in countries such as the Netherlands and Belgium is that it is expected to adhere to a government policy for which the concept of professionalism is entirely focused on neo-liberal priorities: individual success, the restriction of knowledge, profit maximisation, etc., so that any attempt by educational programmes to address issues such as sustainability, social design or hacking are destined to remain marginal efforts at best.

Even a socially engaged practice is still too much focused on itself and/or finds no concrete connection to the everyday context (the social context / citizenship). Critical artists too often marginalise themselves or fail to seek connections within the variety of networks of which they are already contextually and logically a part. The activities of an artistic practice should be more grounded in reality, and focus on being part of a community rather than on being 'professional'.

This is also an important point of concern for ruangrupa. As the organisation and its members become accepted within a professional semi-alternative art scene, they will enjoy increased recognition and status, but there is a danger that the programmes may increasingly become little more than interesting-looking projects. This will be a major challenge for the following generation of ruangrupa members who are now gradually taking over: whether to choose to further build upon previous accomplishments, or to find new challenges, new urgencies and new means of expression.

2.7.2 Making visible also-valid approaches

and

2.7.3 Building networks, connecting

For ruangrupa, making visible and learning from other approaches, other ways of thinking and doing things has always been an important condition for ongoing development as well as for finding suitable collaborative partners. For some, this is important in order to develop ethical values on a practical basis, for example by focusing on alternative forms of collective ownership.[49] Others simply wish to make visible other possible realities, and/or to receive feedback on their own activities, to position themselves among other idiosyncratic characters within and outside the art world. The next step is then to start thinking about building networks in order to strengthen each other's qualities and potential on a local as well as global level.

2.7.4 Empowerment

Another building block of gLEAP is providing a place for different views and ways of doing things, also-valid ideas, and helping inspire confidence that different realities are possible and do indeed exist. An important element of an also-space is to be open to these other realities, to learn from them in order to foster your own practice, or simply being in contact with a number of original individuals or groups.

Empowerment in this context means: seeing and supporting other realities, connecting the artist's own challenges and urgencies to those of others by observing, simply being active, through exchange and respect... A mutual and ongoing process from which a gLEAP practice develops its 'notes' and its 'moments'.

49 See for example Casco's project 'We Are the Time Machines: Time and Tools for Commoning'. *http://cascoprojects.org/we-are-the-time-machines-time-and-tools-for-commoning*

Insert #1 to Chapter 2

A closer look at a number of ruangrupa's platforms and projects.

1 OK. Video: video as a place

The first platform I will be examining here is the festival OK. Video, which has been taking place since 2003. OK. Video is an excellent demonstration of how the medium of video can be seen as a place, somewhere you can hang around the way you hang around on Facebook or on YouTube. OK. Video sees video more as a social medium, rather than as a purely technical medium suitable to experimentation and 'pushing boundaries' as it is usually seen in European media festivals.

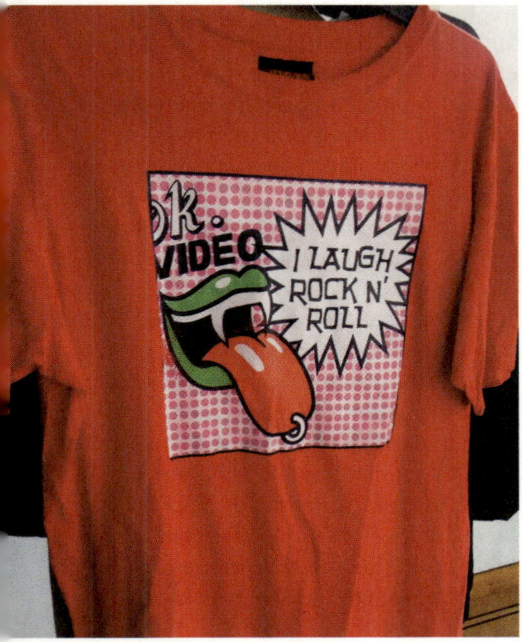

From its first edition onwards OK. Video has always functioned as an art biennale, an infrastructure for local and international production and networking, where video and more generally digital media are applied from a social-critical perspective, and from the perspective of their presence in public spaces, on the streets of the city. This is why I like to say that video can be a place.

Video, in the context of Jakarta, is just as unavoidable as traffic jams in the city, the overabundance of shopping malls, the endless visual stimuli of advertising and other text messages. For better or for worse, video plays a fundamental role in the living environment and personal space of the city's residents. Countless people interact on a daily basis with video/digital images. Video is thus a place where social interaction takes place.

> *'Not so much the technical abilities, as in the early video art are to be experimented, but its presence around people's daily gestures/ habits is of importance or its invisible purposes.'*
> *Ronny Augustinus (co-founder of ruangrupa and founder of the independent publishing house Marjin Kiri) in the catalogue of the first edition of OK. Video, 2003.*

Understanding video as a place can help us see more clearly how we are being seduced, and can also be used to generate a more specific engagement. Since the contemporary use of video (and photography) is characterised by an unprecedented volume of production on professional, amateur and social levels, we could say that understanding video as a place can challenge us to see and interpret the application of the medium in new ways. This is important if OK. Video wishes to remain meaningful as a festival.

An enlightening example in this respect was the programme 'Digital Viral', part of the festival OK. Video FLESH 2011. The exhibition in a sense became the video itself. Rather than a collection of separate works by a number of video artists, or the combination of the different parts being presented as the curator's work, everyone who contributed was a part of the total image, everyone was an element of the video – not only as maker and audience, but also as participant to this mostly social medium. The exhibition challenged artists to redefine their position within the visual process. (For more information on the programme 'Digital Viral', see section 2.6.2 of the main text of the present chapter.)

The programme OK. Video Militia (2007) used video to provide communities (in the traditional sense of the word) with a means of registering their own histories/narratives, whether fictional or nonfictional. In this festival, video was used to bring people together, to allow them to be simultaneously maker and audience. The following text excerpts from the programme catalogue show how OK. Video Militia was a good example of how video can function as a place:

> *'The main reasons for starting the festival is coming together, to give opportunity to the public to use video to challenge the hegemony of the audio-visual language (in the context of the media-hegemony of private companies as for example Fox-media, Bakri-media, SBS-media [...]'*
> *'OK.militia developed video workshops in fifteen locations in twelve cities.'*
> *'Currently, easy access of audio-visual technology is a starting point for collective learning, that nothing is singular, that all things can offer diverse choices.'*

This OK. Video edition provided communities with video as a resource for registering their ideas, as a way of distributing their own narratives and knowledge. What was particularly interesting about this project was the fact that the videos were made by the subjects themselves, rather than with the assistance of NGOs or other such organisations. NGOs are not used to putting the camera, let alone the editing, in the hands of the subjects themselves.

All 120 videos that were made during the various workshops were presented as one large installation in an exhibition space. The exhibition (only) provided a documentary insight of what had been produced and consumed. The final archive of the videos produced refers to a tradition of oral history, and provides the visual dimension of the installation. Or, as the introduction text of the first OK. Video festival (2003) stated: *'The event is considered as a cultural strategy, essentially finding relevance in cultural tradition.'*

The artists' initiative akumassa, a production centre focusing on making videos together with communities, can be seen as a successor to the OK. Video Militia festival, as well as a logical continuation of the experiences and insights gained during this festival, while ruangrupa's ArtLab has further built upon the network brought together by the Militia festival; see for example the project Gerobak Bioskop (Cinema Cart). OK. Video also wishes to influence galleries and collectors. Thus the festival is not only a screening and meeting place, but also sees itself as a necessary instigator of new and/or existing platforms.

OK. Video works from the perspective of everyday/consumer use of the medium in order to generate engagement, to discover possible (new) uses, to strengthen social relationships. The festival was first set up with the goal of providing a platform, by artists and for artists, where colleagues could gain experience and research what might be achieved using the medium. In 2007 the medium of video was used to collaborate with local residents, at the level of user = maker + public. In its current incarnation OK. Video is once again a festival for and by artists, much as it was in its early years.

The question is now whether OK. Video will be able to take the next step and really provide a digital environment that proposes solutions for working with the material in a more independent fashion. Will the platform be able to provide effective resources for a new generation of urban youth, allowing them to design their own digital environment in a fundamentally different, collective way? Particularly in relation to a recurring theme within this book, 'from hot to something else', I find myself wondering whether OK. Video will indeed be able to provide such resources.

> *'In 2001 – between the fall of Suharto in 1998 and the first OK. Video festival in 2003 – Ugeng T. Moetidjo and myself [Hafiz Rancajale] did research about video as an art form in Indonesia. We wondered if there was a certain kind of media awareness amongst artists using video. We were interested in finding artists who gave counterweight to the uncontested stream of electric light in the*

daily life of Jakartans. A large number of students made short films, encouraged by the Konfiden festival. These videos were related more to short films and to television language. Ugeng and I found there was a lack of alternative or artistic expression within the use of video and film language. Taking the consequences of the research, ruangrupa felt the need to create a platform and network to give an alternative for critical expression with the medium of video. Our aim was to explore the possibilities of video among the members of ruangrupa. We wanted to set up a festival that could make a connection with young people through free space and art. The festival should be related to a present-day urban culture to attract and seduce young people to think about the nature of the "given" medium of video. "OK. Video Jakarta International Video Art Festival" became the full name of the festival. It incorporates the language of the young generation. The title is taken from the album "OK Computer" by Radiohead. "Video Art Festival" points out that this is an art form and that we wanted to talk about and explore video art. "International" shows our need to build the festival as a network, a place to exchange ideas, not only locally.'
Hafiz Rancajale, in a conversation with me about the origins of the festival, 2013.

Some typical characteristics of OK. Video are:

- Working within: working from a direct involvement with that which already exists, making decisions and determining one's further direction from this perspective.
- Shifting positions: the relative position and relationship between makers, users and public is not one-dimensional. What exactly is the position of the professional practitioner?
- Networks: setting up platforms, strengthening networks, exerting influence.
- Education: getting to know the medium of video, thus gaining insight into the power of media as well as a better understanding of the city, often through workshops.

2 A biennale is not a generic place

How to relate to a situation or context that has no specific connection to your own (local) context? Fiction, more fiction, too much reality, too much science... Dreams: icons for hope. Fiction, because reality/history is never one-dimensional. Fiction is an essential element of popular visual culture.

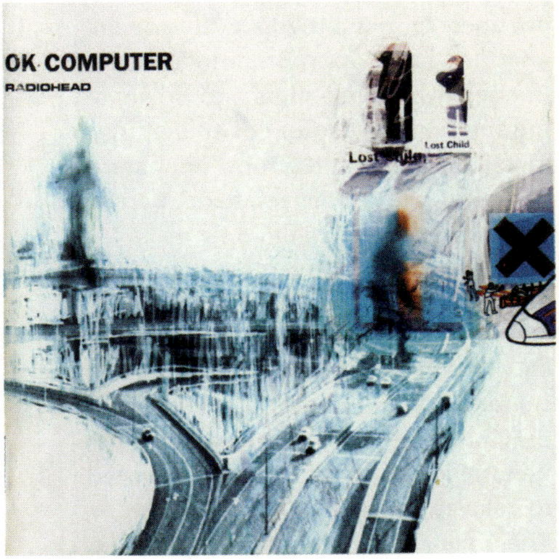

What is the possible relevance of presenting something in an art biennale in a way that engages with the local context and at the same time also involves one's own context? Ruangrupa's contributions to the 2005 Istanbul Biennial and the 2012-2013 Asia Pacific Triennial of Contemporary Art in Brisbane, Australia are examples of a process of contextually logical thinking and acting.

At the Istanbul Biennial, ruangrupa wanted to find a way of linking the cities of Jakarta and Istanbul on an equal footing. Both cities are located in so-called emerging economies, both share the typical characteristics of a booming megalopolis, and both are home to a large population of citizens from 'lower' socio-economic classes, many of whom have recently arrived from the countryside in search of better prospects. The romanticism of a working class that resigns itself to its fate while still dreaming of a prosperous future, if not for themselves then at least for their children and grandchildren.

Ruangrupa presented two iconic and somewhat similar figures, one from each city, that embodied these hopes, dreams and longings: Benjamin and Kemal Sunal. Both are comedy actors, much beloved for the sympathetic characters they portray in their movies (incidentally, both died of a heart attack, one during a football match and the other during a plane trip). Ruangrupa used visual products and visual language that are specific to the media of television and film, by re-appropriating iconic images from these films and presenting them in the context of an inspiring installation and in the form of posters, badges, T-shirts, stickers, texts, banners, videos, etc. The installation was designed to resemble the gift shop of an old cinema house or pop music venue.

Within just a few weeks, ruangrupa selected the local iconic figure Kemal Sunal and put together the installation, bringing from Jakarta only the general idea and the materials related to Jakarta's own local hero Benjamin. The ability to improvise thus played an important role in this project. Working and collecting materials on location is often difficult; projects thus often tend to end up with merely illustrative images, or they lack a real connection to the local context.

'The Kuda' was a fiction put together by ruangrupa for the 2012-2013 Asia Pacific Triennial of Contemporary Art in Brisbane, Australia. This is a work that really needed to be experienced, preferably in person. Since I was not fortunate enough to encounter the work in this fashion, I will cite here the Indonesian curator and writer Alia Swastika:

'- a. Just been listening to a good radio documentary (or mockumentary?) about the 1970s Indonesian punk band The Kuda - whether they even existed is sketchy and in fact after a bit of digging looks like it might be a fictional band used by Jakarta art collective ruangrupa as a vehicle to discuss Indonesia and punk in Joh Bjelke-Petersen's Brisbane in the 1970s (who infamously even

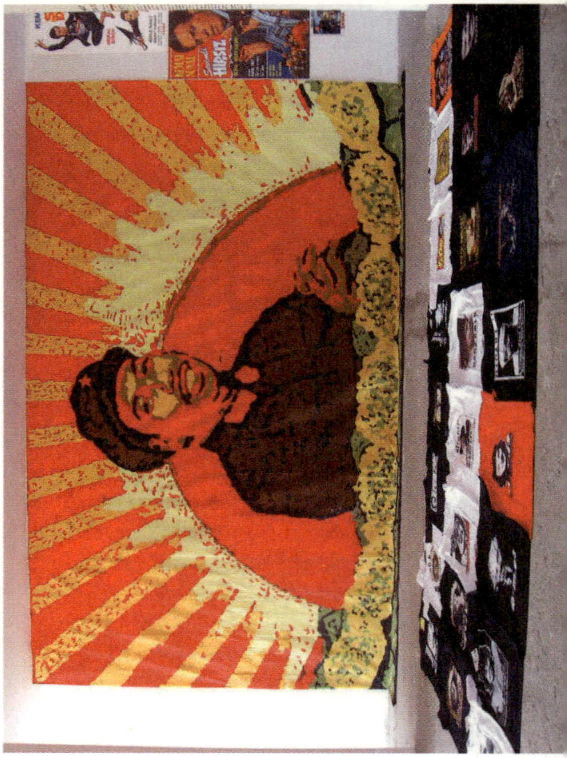

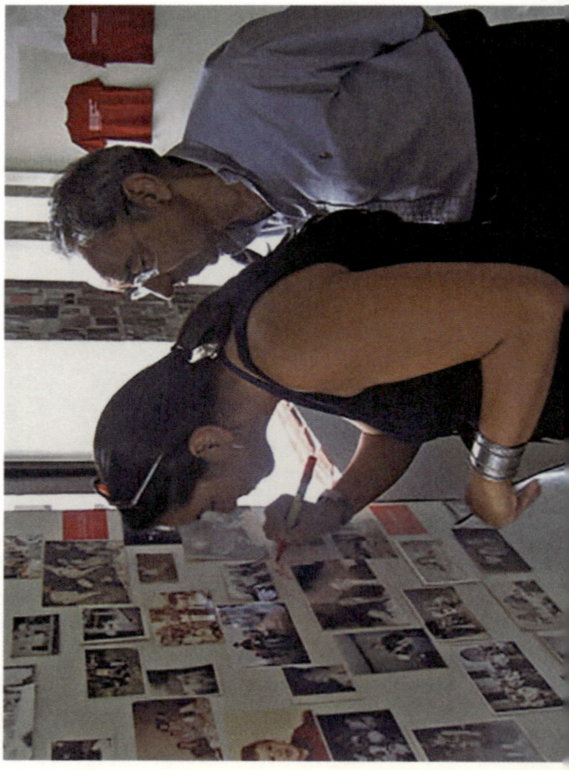

had a special branch of police to harass punks).
'Whatever the truth, the program still covers much of interest though, with interviews with members of The Saints, The Go-Betweens, and Xero, as well as the roots of Indonesian punk within the context of rock in Suharto's Indonesia. It was broadcast on Australia's ABC Radio National Hindsight program and you can stream it here or download it.
(http://subcultatlas.blogspot.nl)
'- b. For the opening night, Ruang Rupa invited legendary Brisbane band The Family Butcher to perform. Inspired by punk music in Brisbane in the '70s, when bands like the Saints, the Go-Betweens and radio stations like 4ZZZ were active, Ruang Rupa linked the Brisbane music scene to the history of an imaginary Indonesian band called The Kuda.
'At first sight, visitors wouldn't even realize that The Kuda is a fictional story, as Ruang Rupa has done an amazing job to create the fictional band displaying artifacts as proof of their existence.
'Through the imaginary band, Ruang Rupa investigates what happened in Indonesia during the '70s, in particular examining popular culture and its social political context. The invented Kuda band was presented as significant to Jakarta's music scene and becoming part of the young people's movement in the early days of Suharto's regime.
'Ruang Rupa shows how The Kuda lived through a period of transition in Indonesia and how they built a strong connection with the people in the city. Video documentaries, interviews, and research on the development of pop-culture in Indonesia stand side by side with make-believe interviews of prominent figures who talk about the band's importance. Working in collaboration with local artist Fintan Magee, Ruang Rupa have created a huge mural installed in the lobby of the museum. Also on display are items considered historically important: cassette tapes, song notes, clothes, posters, magazines, archival footage – anything a rock group living in the '70s may have collected over the years. The most visible object is the Vespa scooter "used" by the group during that time. To give a better context of the Indonesian music scene, the artist collective also set up music stations where visitors can hear rock music from the 1970s.
'Rather than talking only about music, Ruang Rupa's main focus in this project is the subject of history. They explore the thin line between reality and fake, how history can be traced through daily phenomenon and how the history also influenced the life of common people.'
Alia Swastika, the Jakarta Globe, January 12, 2013.

Connecting various contexts plays an important role in the work of ruangrupa. In international projects this means seeking connections between locations:

> *'Brisbane's youth were marching the streets against the increasingly draconian laws of the Bjelke-Petersen government, while their contemporaries in Jakarta were frequently engaged in street battles with the army during years of the Soeharto regime. While Brisbane and Jakarta may appear to be very different places on the surface, they were literally linked by the spirit of rock and punk, providing the soundtrack to a generation in revolt.'*
> *Australian Broadcasting Corporation, 'Search for the Kuda', summary of a radio programme with a link to the content, December 9, 2012. http://www.abc.net.au/radionational/programs/hindsight/kuda/4408130*

How did the project come into being, and how was it implemented?

> *'For example for this APT project, I already forgot whose idea this is, it's just like one body, and luckily in ruangrupa, we are all very different but we all respect each other, our skills and knowledge, even our stupidity, it's really organic. [...] Both the Singapore Fiction (Singapore Biennale 2011) and the especially the APT work, as we went into history, even for us we learned a lot, shaking our belief as well toward the history, while making and processing this project, which has been really interesting. We always think that it's important to put our position or approach in a tension between art and not-art that*

is coming out through playfulness and parody, it's coming from there.'
Interview with ruangrupa by Paul Andrew, Saturday, December 15, 2012, http://paulandrew-interviews.blogspot.nl

Some typical characteristics of ruangrupa operating within an international art circuit:

- Connecting contexts: being in dialogue is usually only meaningful when there is some degree of personal engagement. This is why it is important to find common ground.
- Fiction is a powerful instrument, an effective element for addressing the imagination of a (non-specialist) public and for bringing currently relevant topics to life.
- Starting and formulating projects: ruangrupa speaks as one artist. Ongoing activity without much individual claim for credit.
- Popular culture and activism: using easily recognisable media (such as video and stickers) makes it easier to make connections, to call attention to your topics, and to provide a point of entry to other perspectives besides the mainstream; other also-ways of thinking and seeing things.

3 Jakarta 32°C

Jakarta 32°C, which has been taking place since 2004, is a bi-annual art manifestation where students from Jakarta's various universities participate in a collective exhibition project.

Jakarta 32°C originated out of a curiosity as to what students on the campuses were doing and talking about, and what their dreams were. After a number of meetings between students and members of ruangrupa to discuss a possible collaborative effort with and within the educational institutions, the eventual participants decided to continue the discussion outside these institutions and to set up an independent platform. The Jakarta 32°C biennale provides students from all universities in Jakarta with an opportunity to collectively formulate and implement projects, which are almost by definition multidisciplinary and collaborative. Essentially, Jakarta 32°C makes connections in the city, builds networks and highlights the importance of the presence of a certain critical mass in a city of some 15 million residents – a city where commercial real estate as well as religious and governmental infrastructures occupy a great deal of the available public space. The format and scope of the biennale means that ruangrupa is able to establish certain activities within the city, however minimal in the greater scheme of things, and to promote other ways of thinking within a broader agenda. The biennale is a large-scale event with an opening evening in the Galeri Nasional, with music events, a young stylish crowd, etc.

At festivals or biennales such as these, the various roles or positions are mostly clearly defined. The public is expected to come and look at the works or to see someone working (or at the most, to participate in someone's project). Jakarta 32°C consciously and unconsciously gives a different twist to these positions: for example, the makers are also part of the public. It's interesting to observe the active or passive role of audience members within the spectacle. Students from various institutes are introduced to the main theme and the various sub-programmes through a number of workshops and presentations. In 2012, a number of communities from Jakarta played a role in setting up and supervising the projects. Thus:

- Participating students are the makers as well as the organisers of their own festival.
- Participating students are part of the public, since the large quantity of projects inevitably positions their own contributions next to that of other participants.
- Participating students are also an audience for the communities involved.

The Jakarta 32°C biennale shows us that it is possible for artists or groups of artists to find and engage their public in a more conscious manner. The students are also a potential public for ruangrupa. Rather than orchestrating large-scale publicity campaigns or using big managerial instruments in order to present a purely consumptive event, ruangrupa chooses instead to directly involve the students, to encourage them to express their qualities and to connect these with already-present alternative entities in the city.

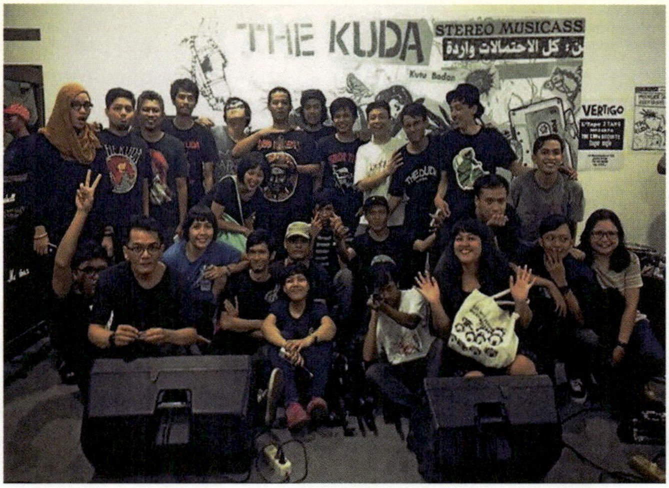

ruangrupa

THE KUDA

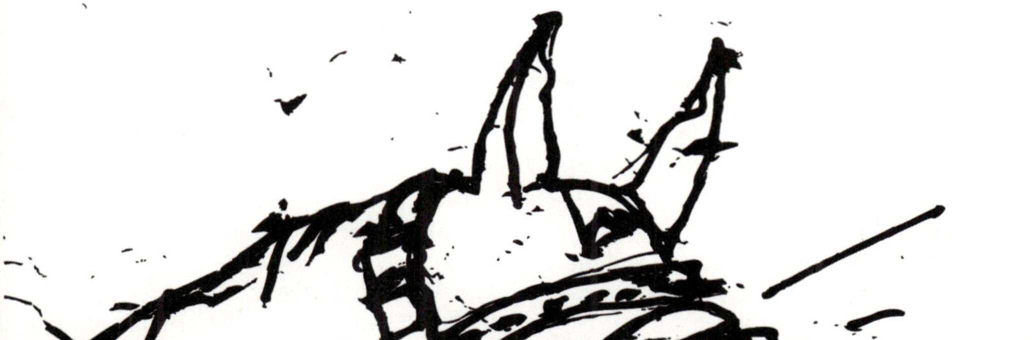

THE UNTOLD STORY OF

INDONESIAN UNDERGROUND MUSIC IN THE 70'S

The biennale is a showcase of the energy that can be encountered in the city, of communities, of an art community in Jakarta in general. It is a platform for getting to know each other, for finding out what students are up to and for connecting with that which is already going on.

However, the 2014 edition of the biennale was a bit too much about the art itself and the production of work on location, without really focusing on the context or the location. Perhaps the biennale was running a bit on autopilot that year, and it would be a good idea now to allow Jakarta 32°C to function more independently, and to really transfer control to a new generation of ruangrupa members.

Curiosity generates new activities and insights about one's own activities:

- The role of the public
- Casting light on the presence of a specific scene
- Finding and involving in your programme a potential public as well as interesting communities
- Setting up platforms

4 Stiker Kota

The collective memory of the city and the narratives of the 'lower' socio-economic classes as a concrete product.

Stiker Kota is a book, a catalogue of stickers found and bought at various locations in the city. The collection is the result of a number of projects on the topic of urban printing as a visual expression which a 'lower' socio-economic class identifies with. Urban printing is defined as the production of stickers, embroideries, posters, T-shirts, banners, murals, etc. For example, T-shirts of a pop idol such as Benjamin (see section #2 in this insert on the Istanbul Biennial, 'A biennale is not a generic place'), stickers with a religious text, posters of a dangdut singer, etc. Urban printing is a constant source of inspiration for members of ruangrupa, and Stiker Kota is a compilation of stickers collected on the streets during a period of some 15 years. The book is a reflection of a cultural manifestation that is gradually disappearing from the streetscape. The collection of images brings together a visual representation of dreams, hopes, etc. and provides a powerful survey of a variety of cultures. This also helps provide a better understanding of ruangrupa's contribution to the Istanbul Biennial: casting a light on the fictions/narratives present in the city through the 'Kuda' project.

Stiker Kota is an archive, an overview of the collective memory of a city:

- Perhaps the book could have been even better with some outside help on a technical and editorial level. On the other hand it might have then become too theoretical, too much of a formal study or a lifestyle book. And precisely somewhere between these two poles is where the work of ruangrupa often takes place. Sometimes a bit of a pity, but often very fortunately, since what ruangrupa does is less about representation and more about active involvement.
- Ruangrupa collects narratives in the city. These are collected among the 'lower' socio-economic classes. Often ruangrupa presents these exactly as they were found, or takes them as a starting point for original artworks. Either way, the materials are used 'as is', in a direct fashion and without making them too 'artistic'.

5 RURU Gallery

RURU Gallery a public platform for young artists and curators, as well as a meeting place. There is a real need to provide a place for young people, to allow them to develop and test their vocabulary. This is an important characteristic of many artists or artistic communities in Indonesia. The function of the gallery has changed throughout the years, but the aspect of dialogue has always been present. Currently this is mostly a dialogue between young artists and curators on making exhibitions together, whereas in the past this dialogue often had to do with discussions on cultural concepts; there was a film evening that often focused on specific target audiences, there were workshops, incidental events, etc.

Ruangrupa itself doesn't really need this gallery. Why even call it a 'gallery' in the first place, when ruangrupa's artistic practice is really about something else?

- The word 'gallery' is a way to efficiently communicate with the outside world.
- The word 'gallery' is also a way (in the Indonesian context) of making sure the public takes the platform seriously. It provides young artists with an activity that is taken seriously, that provides a certain prestige (in the past, ruangrupa was often seen as a group of young people that weren't really serious about their work).
- Using the word 'gallery' also inspires a certain focus and concentration on the part of the artist. The concentration necessary to write a text, to work on an effective communication, to think more about the presentation, about who to invite, etc.
- Providing an independent space for young artists and curators to try things out. Providing the know-how present in the RURU Gallery.
- Due to a lack of other non-commercial spaces in Jakarta, there is a need for a (more or less) neutral space for different kinds of artists.
- Supporting the work of female curators and artists.

In other words, calling it a 'gallery' helps to create a productive tension and also to fill a gap in the cultural landscape.

However, the programme is currently too broad and too general. Now would be a good time to reconsider the function of RURU Gallery, to reformulate its function and its possibilities. Recently the focus has been on emerging artists of whichever discipline. If the gallery is to be given a new function in the new reorganisation of the house, there will be a challenge in formulating this function in a different way now that the house is more or less taking on the appearance of an office and of the clothing and souvenir shops located nearby. Currently there are three members who occasionally discuss the future of the gallery. At some point this discussion will naturally take place within a broader circle, when the time is right, after a number of viewpoints have been formulated. It's not as though a concept will be formulated and then rolled out and implemented, that's simply not the way ruangrupa functions.

Providing a place and sharing your experiences and insights with a younger generation of artists:

- The concept of a 'gallery' is applied, not so much for the sake of having a gallery, but rather as an instrument for stimulating artists and for providing them visibility and credibility.
- This presupposes a different function for the public, for interpreting what they see, for the way in which discussions take place.
- An open attitude, rather than understanding art according to a specific definition and dividing artistic practices into fixed categories.
- Strengthening the artistic climate.

'[...] not only Ruru, but also Javanese artists' initiatives in general relate first and foremost to the community. In a political climate where there is little to no government support for the arts, they function as organic structures that read social change and work best when boundaries between art and non-art are blurred. They change and their public changes with them.'
Sanne Oorthuizen, 'Happy Birthday Ruangrupa', Metropolis M, January 27, 2011. http://metropolism.com/features/happy-birthday-ruangrupa/english

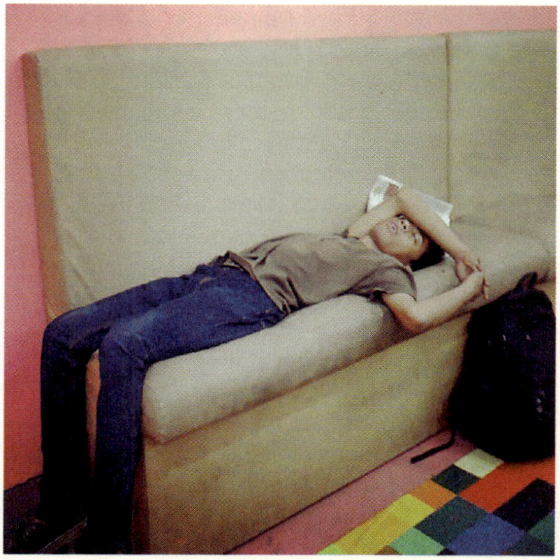

6 Ruangrupa and educational outreach as a platform

An artistic practice can be understood as an ongoing process of learning, transferring knowledge, sharing experiences. Educational outreach has always been a consistent element within the programme of ruangrupa and of many other artists' initiatives in Indonesia. For example, in the functions of Jakarta 32°C and the RURU Gallery.

Educational outreach is about a generous structure: not only helping others, but also developing yourself and establishing connections that can then go on to help each other. It should be clear by now that educational outreach is very much a part of ruangrupa's DNA. Currently ruangrupa is considering how these educational elements could be presented more clearly and coherently. However, since educational outreach already plays such an important role in ruangrupa's programme, I asked some members why they felt the need to create a separate platform specifically for this purpose. I didn't really get a clear answer to this question.

There is an obvious tendency on an international level to consider art and educational outreach as one single theme. In the context of the platform Arts Collaboratory, of which ruangrupa is one of 23 participating organisations, this is a clearly defined concept for formulating a collective project, from which the idea of 'Art Schoolaboratory' arose. It is certainly a good idea to compile an overview of the educational elements from the various activities; there is also an effort to find out whether it is a good idea to set up an official curriculum based on these elements. Within the framework of the collaboration with Arts Collaboratory, an 'Art Schoolaboratory' project will be set up at three different locations, each in their own context and each with their own way of doing things. After a certain period of time, the idea is to rotate the programmes. This is important if we are really serious about relating to our context, which should not take place exclusively in the neighbourhood where we live; we have been existing within a (g)local context for some time now, and this applies to artists and activists as well as to multinationals and political institutions. In this context we as artists must think further than merely showing our work at biennales or maintaining an international professional network. It is perhaps more important to establish long-term connections, to cultivate relationships and to share our experience and knowledge, to actively connect local activities toward forging a broader movement.

Ruangrupa might consider this following step as a core element for its future programme. Ruangrupa has always sought and maintained strong connections with communities within the city of Jakarta and the island of Java, and in a broader context within South East Asia and Europe; examples of this are ruangrupa's 10th anniversary event Decompression #10 (see section 2.3.2.3 of the main text of the present chapter, example 3) and more specifically the programme ruru.net in the context of this event.

By participating in the Bienal de São Paulo, ruangrupa has now further expanded its international network to include South America. In a society in which national boundaries are increasingly seen as fictions by multinationals, why shouldn't they be equally understood as fictions by contextual art practices such as ruangrupa's?

Either way, all of this provides an interesting case study to see how these types of educational outreach programmes can connect and strengthen each other, and it will be interesting to see whether Art Schoolaboratory succeeds in going further than merely sharing each other's curriculum.

- Generous structure: making yourself available to share and to go on learning.
- Connecting networks across national boundaries.
- Educational outreach: this is part of the DNA of Indonesian artists and artists initiatives, see for example the concept of Sanggar as defined in section 2.2.3.2 of the main text of the present chapter, 'Indonesian customs that have shaped ruangrupa'.
- Experimenting with official systems: what does it mean to attempt to offer an educational outreach programme that is as official or as thorough as possible, and how can we make this happen?

Insert #2 to Chapter 2

LATEST NEWS: the nearby institutional future

The formal and informal activities taking place in the ruangrupa house at Tebet Timur Dalam Raya No. 6 have become increasingly difficult to manage. The balance between the domestic and public function of the house has gradually become confused. It's becoming increasingly difficult to work in the house itself. Computers have been stolen, there are too many guests coming and going, too many distractions, the library and video storage are too vulnerable for this situation, and so on. Users and visitors have lost the sense of ownership of the space.

A preliminary decision was made to split the house in two, with a public space in the front and an office space in the back, in a sense more a members-only space. The Ruru Shop became a shop with its own front door. Either way, it was clear that the structure of ruangrupa needed to be redesigned, and that the 'house' situation had gradually become unsustainable. The structural change is part of an ongoing adaptation of ruangrupa's mode of organisation and maintenance. The aftermath of the 2015 Jakarta Biennale, with which ruangrupa was closely involved, provided an opportunity or a trigger to relocate ruangrupa in the main venue of the Biennale.

The present publication was researched and written from the perspective of ruangrupa's evolution from its early beginnings until around 2014. In the meantime ruangrupa has taken a major next step, which we could describe as going from a 'nongkrong'-based practice to a 'lumbung' (rice barn) system. I have previously described nongkrong as a way of sitting together, chatting informally and allowing a programme to develop from there. Lumbung, on the other hand, refers to the way rice is stored by a community (family or village)*. In the context of the new step being taken by ruangrupa, lumbung could be understood in terms of the ecosystem of a larger community of which ruangrupa is a part. Other organisations participating in this ecosystem are Forum Lenteng, Serrum and Grafis Huru-Hara, as well as the ruangrupa platforms OK. Video and Jakarta 32°C.

This new Gudang Sarinah Ekosistem community is part of the next logical step toward further collectivism and creating a specific new institutional space, with a focus on caring and sustaining each other based on one's own strengths and capacities. Or, as artist/curator Ade Darmawan wrote in an e-mail to me (May 17, 2016): *'Each organization then should think about both ways: about themself and also about the others or as a whole ecosystem.'*

How exactly this vision will manifest itself in practice is quite unpredictable of course, and well beyond the scope of the present publication. However I felt it necessary to at least briefly touch upon these ongoing developments.

The focus for this new step is mainly internal: how to work together as a group of organisations, how to set up a structure that makes it possible to fully support each other's programme, including a shared budget. Within a few years we will see what this new structure has brought to ruangrupa and to the Gudang Sarinah Ekosistem community.

An interesting experiment in the transition towards this new structure is the exhibition 'SuperSub' where Ade Darmawan invited members of various Indonesian/Javanese artists' collectives (of which some are part of the new 'Ekosistem') to work together:

> *'According to Darmawan the exhibition title refers to soccer world terminology. Here a "super substitute" characterizes a soccer player put in the game to change its direction. In the same way Darmawan has brought together a group of artists that are all game*

changers within the collective. SuperSub – on collectivism explores themes like cultural exchange, social engagement, and artistic process.'
Den Frie Centre of Contemporary Art, 'SuperSub – on collectivism', 2016. *http://en.denfrie.dk/portfolio-item/supersub-on-collectivism*

For more information on the Gudang Sarinah Ekosistem community, see *http://gudangsarinah.com*. See also below a flyer made in 2016 to introduce the new space.

** 'In an attempt to make the museum concept less foreign, I explained that a museum is similar to a local cultural form, the lumbung or rice barn. In my visits to Kenyah villages during the first survey, I became intrigued by the lumbung because they are not only used to store rice, but frequently also house and protect a family's heirlooms. I also learned that lumbung embody a number of indigenous, preventive conservation principles and techniques. Here conservation is used in the museological sense as any action taken to protect objects from damage or to control or prevent their deterioration. For example, lumbung are generally located outside the village and on high ground where they can be protected from fires and flooding.'*

Christina Faye Kreps, Liberating Culture: Cross-cultural Perspectives on Museums, Curation, and Heritage Preservation, Psychology Press, 2003.

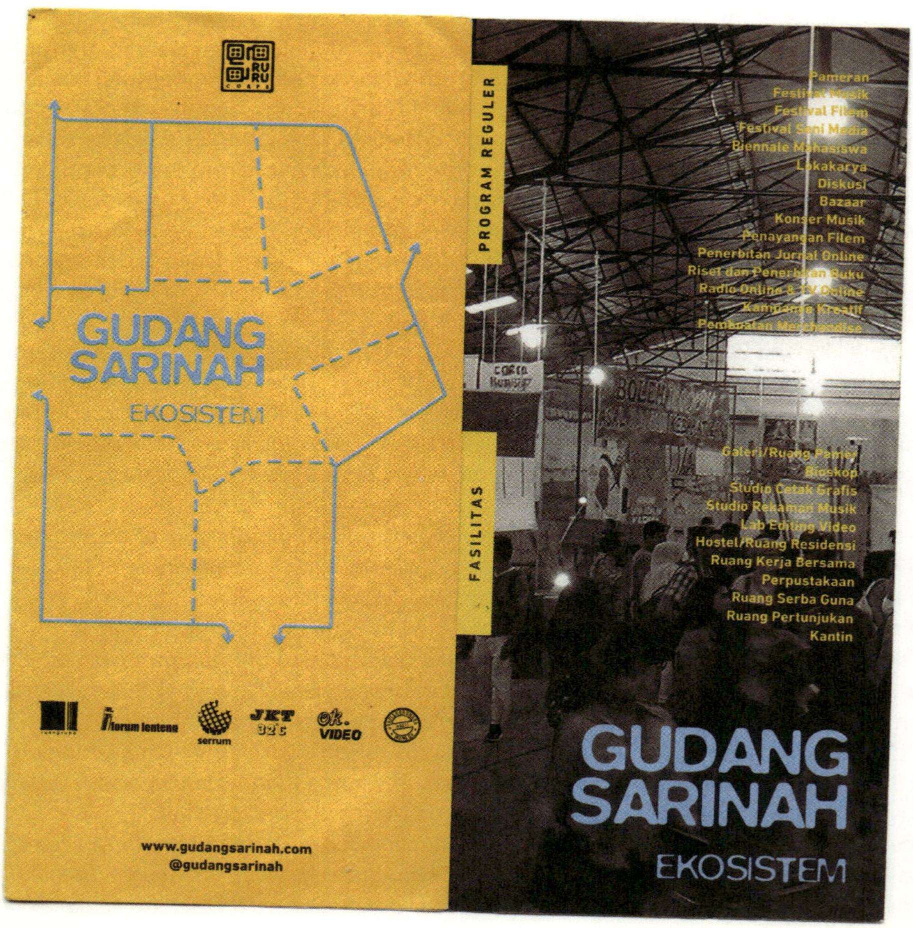

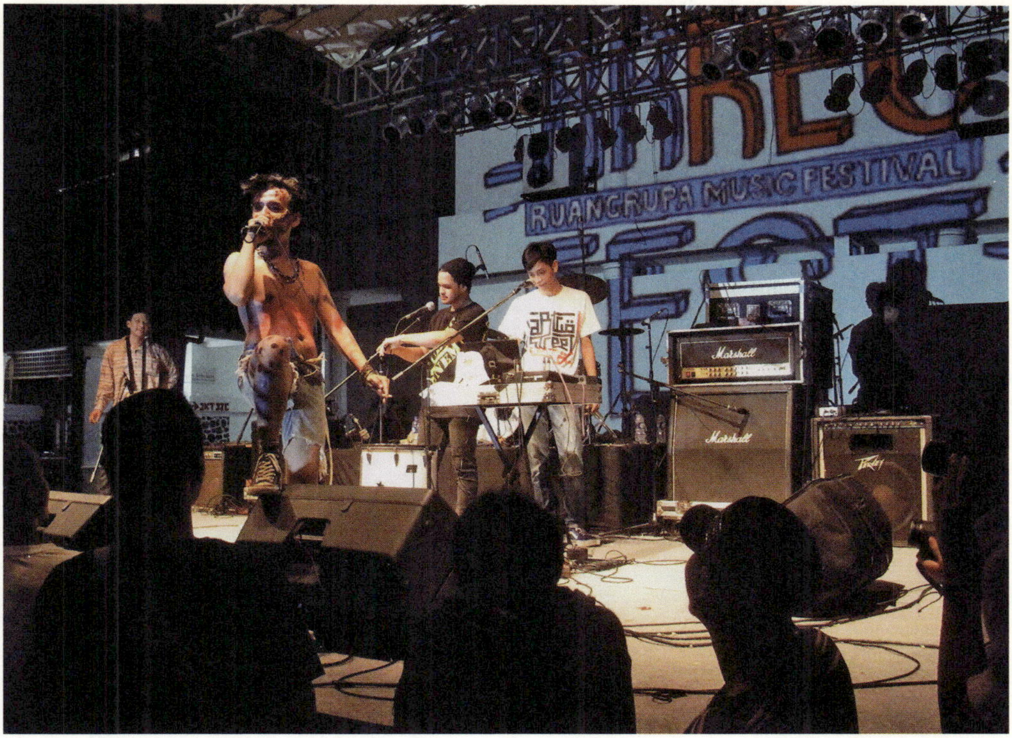

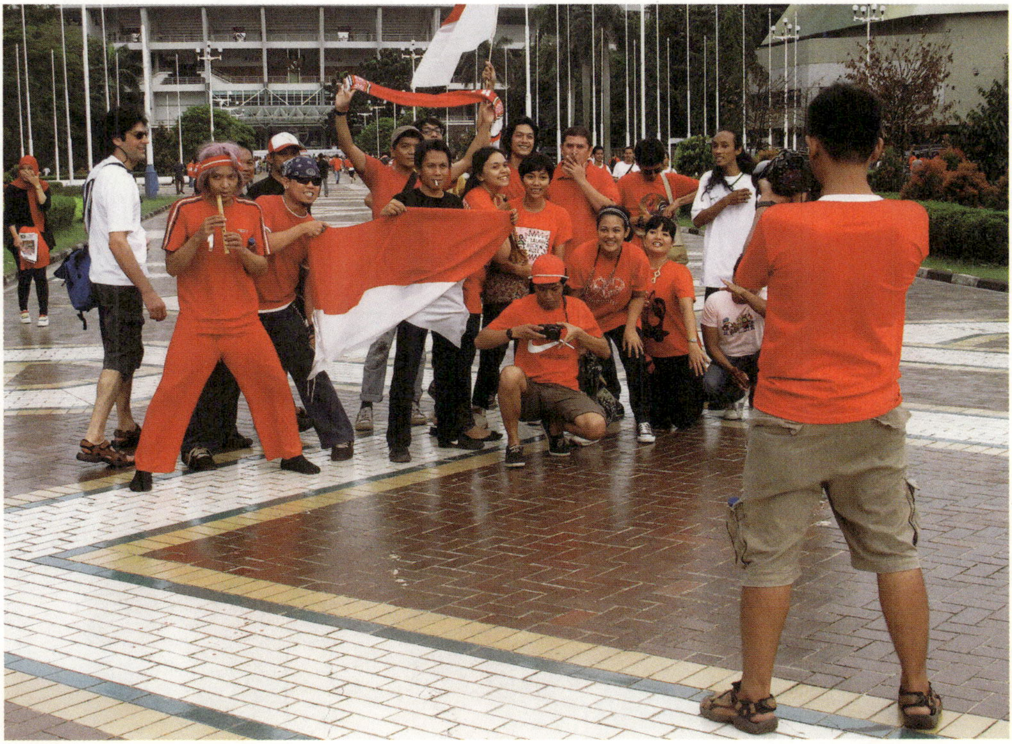

Ruangrupa, an artists' initiative from Jakarta, Indonesia

If an artist produces a body of work which is about a critique of society, about the citizen who is in need. Artists often talk about the citizen from a specialist zone. A specialist zone is not the same as a neutral zone.

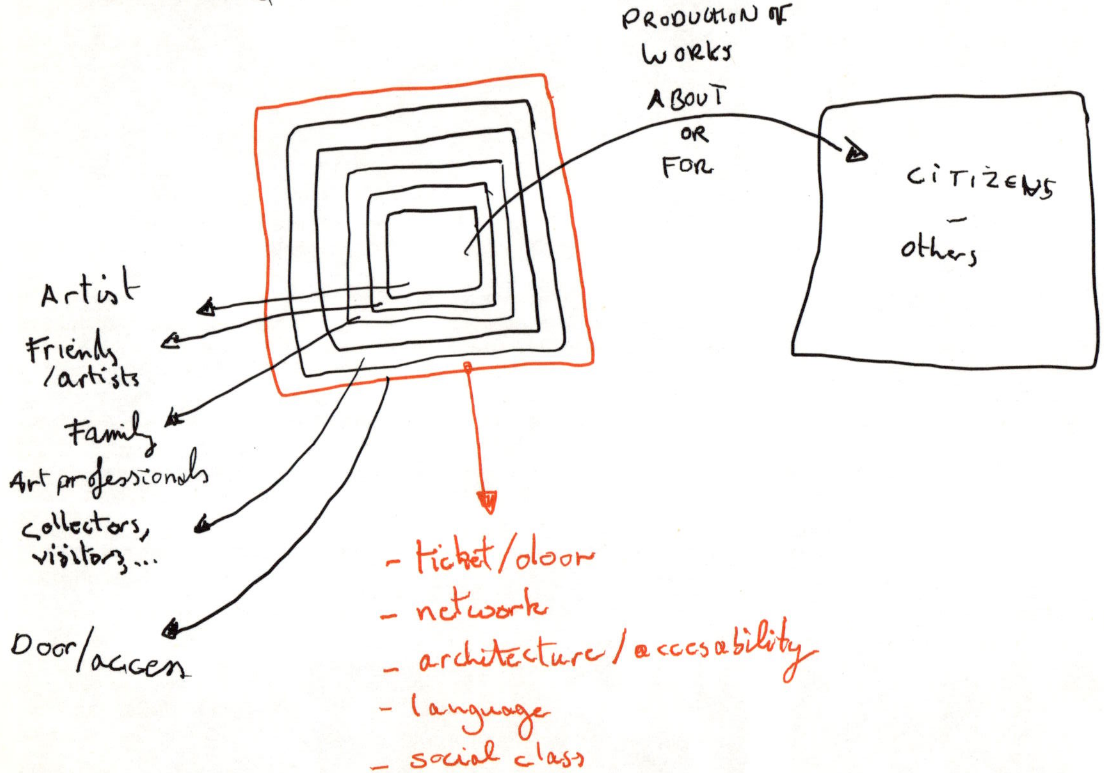

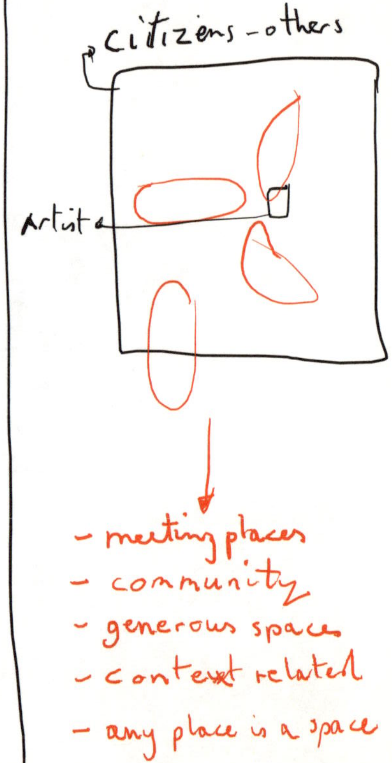

Chapter 3:
From alternative space to also-space

3.1 Also-space as a term and a place

3.1.1 Where does the idea of also-space come from?

In the mid to late 1990s, the term 'non-place' (after M. Augé's book 'Non-Places', 1992) was used in the art world to describe places that were seen as non-productive, leftover spaces, residual and more or less abandoned, transitional spaces in which you might find yourself on your way to someplace else. I found it strange and somewhat passive to label these places as abandoned, or to represent them as non-places in videos, photos and slides (looking back, I can only remember works by Els Opsomer and Aglaia Konrad, though these are by no means the most appropriate examples. The exhibition 'Wasteland' in Rotterdam in 1993 was perhaps a better example of this trend. At the Documenta X, in 1997, there was also some interest in the concept of non-place). At that point in my own development I saw the non-place as an essential cogwheel in the broader system of a 'globalised world'. Naomi Klein described some aspects of this in her book 'No Logo' (2000). Whatever the case, non-places are not residual or marginal spaces, they are in fact places in their own right, and often essential parts of a greater whole.

Much later, in 2009, I spent half a year in Beijing in the context of a residency programme. One thing I missed there was informal spaces for showing art, presentation spaces for dialogue and production. The sheer size of the city, the art boom currently going on and the inevitable focus on success meant that there was less room and less attention for such spaces. There simply seemed to be no time or money to organise them. If they indeed did exist, it was for a public of insiders and anyway everything was in Mandarin, which I didn't speak. Also, all art events that could be seen as more or less alternative were still inevitably focused on the success, image, and production of the individual artist. I assumed there must actually be enough people interested in bringing together dialogue and production in a certain way, but who simply couldn't find the time, or had other reasons for not initiating such a situation.[1] This is why I decided to take the initiative to create such a space. I organised two exhibitions in Beijing for which I used the term 'also-space'.[2]

Occupying space, meeting people, an informal setting in which to share one's work with colleagues and the public; a generous space, partly because it was possible, partly because it was necessary. It was from this perspective that the concept of the also-space for the first time took on a concrete shape for me. These exhibitions were a first step in formulating what an also-space meant to me, and thus how I imagined what for me might be an ideal artistic practice. And now that I've had the opportunity to closely research the Indonesian artists' collective ruangrupa, I understand much better the significance of these exhibitions.

3.1.2 Alternative space vs. also-space

In chapter two of this book, I briefly introduced the also-space as a concept for artists working within existing communities which they are already a part of.

I propose the model of also-space in order to

1 Such places did exist to some extent, or were being set up: examples include HomeShop (which I have already discussed in chapter 1 of this book), Sugar Jar (a shop for noise music and other experimental musics, *http://nytimes.com/2007/10/27/arts/music/27expe.html*) and Forget Art (an intervention-based institution for self-organised projects, focused on relating artistic practices directly to the social context).

2 See *http://vanhoe.org/paginas/alsospace.html*

encourage artists to consider their production from within the different communities they are a part of (artists, neighbours, social class, hobbies, profession, knowledge, etc.), beginning from an ontology of 'being-in-common'. In this way of thinking, there is no need to exclude oneself, no need to protect one's ideas as in the traditional autonomy-based Western models of the arts. Instead we are in constant dialogue, and each individual ego is essentially part of this 'we'.

Today, (critical) citizens such as artists should not make the mistake of isolating themselves in so-called alternative spaces. What they are actually seeking is more likely an 'also-world', an also-possible construction of everyday life. The issues in the arts are the same as in local and global economics: people understand that a substantial change is needed, but the greatest obstacle is always on a cultural level. Referring to economic obstacles, the philosopher and educator Euclides André Mance, a member of the Popular Solidarity Economy Network in Brazil, pointed out that:

> *'However fast solidarity economy is developing, millions of people who fight for "another world" (I use the term "also-world", RV) do not practise or participate in it. First, because they are unaware of it; second, because of the relatively difficult access to the products and services produced within this other economy. Both difficulties can be quickly surmounted. The main obstacle is cultural: to overcome a consumerist culture that prizes quantity, excess, possession and waste over the welfare of people and communities (i.e. the power of the mainstream or centralised world, RV), we need to replace unsustainable forms of production, consumption and ways-of-life with the affirmation of new ways of producing, consuming and living in solidarity.'* [3]

This implies that it is not sufficient to have a 'good' or 'right' concept, but that an engaged practice must be embedded within a long-term commitment. Instead of seeing themselves as the avant-garde of a movement, artists should instead find their place as contributors and collaborators within a movement. By identifying themselves as 'alternative', artists confirm the hegemony of the dominant system, the centralised world.[4] The concept of alternative space is thus inadequate. The term also-space, however, offers possibilities for overcoming the limitations of alternative spaces.

3.2 Also-space: learning from Indonesian artists and art initiatives

In addition to my study of ruangrupa, I have focused on 4 other Indonesian artists and art initiatives. Working together is often normal for artists and other cultural practitioners in Indonesia. By examining other practices, my goal was to confirm the ideas I had formulated while studying ruangrupa.

3.2.1 Why Indonesian examples?

3.2.1.1 In general

First of all, it is important to note that this is a momentary and personal proposal with the goal of understanding:

- how Indonesian artists or collectives often work (whether consciously or not) with the notion of citizenship or 'warga' (the Indonesian translation of 'citizen'/'citizenship');
- how to reconnect the artist's everyday activities with their artistic production. As I like to say: 'it is easier to perform being a rebel than to live as one';
- how to support interesting practices of artists who are lacking recognition. How to support interesting artists or communities when they have no real grip on what they are actually doing;
- how can we practice or teach art without falling into the trap of the mainstream (art) world, which often refers to (critical) concepts such as post-colonial, post-Fordism, art in a global context, activism

[3] Euclides André Mance, 'Solidarity Economics', Instituto de Filosofia da Libertação, 2007, p. 3. *http://solidarius.com.br/mance/biblioteca/turbulence-en.pdf*

[4] A world depicted in the work of Bureau d'études (*http://bureaudetudes.org/*) or Walid Raad, for example in his explanation of the APT (Artists' Pension Trust, see *http://eng.majalla.com/2013/04/article55240387*)

or sustainability, but only produces a *representation* of these themes.
For example, the 2013 Istanbul Biennial was interesting in the context of the Gezi Park protests.[5] However, all the Biennial was able to do was show a romanticised archive of interesting 'activist' artists from the past. Another example: The Amsterdam Stedelijk Museum's project space SMBA has a series of exhibitions titled Global Collaborations: *'Global Collaborations is a three-year project that aims to generate an informed and well-balanced overview of developments in contemporary art from a global perspective. It is based on collaborative partnerships with experimental and multifaceted art institutions throughout the world and encompasses exhibitions, publications, events, and an online platform.'* [6] But how can we talk about real 'collaborative partnerships' when in the end the exhibition remains just that, an exhibition with its back turned to the context of the principles it is supposedly based on?

3.2.1.2 In Indonesia, and Java in particular:

Many artists seem to work with the concept of 'warga' (citizenship) as an integral part of their practice, with the goal of:
– portraying the everyday reality of people and using this as a tool for working beyond political power structures, thus empowering individuals as well as communities (see section 3.3.3, 'Practitioners', artist Moelyono);
– using art as a tool to empower people (see section 3.3.1, 'Practitioners', collective Lifepatch);
– seeing people as collaborators and co-authors (see section 3.3.4, 'Practitioners', artist Wok the Rock);
– gaining access to resources, collaborations, ideas (see section 3.3.2, 'Practitioners', collective Jatiwangi Art Factory);
– being useful or supportive to their fellow artists (see chapter 2, section 2.6, 'Development of ruangrupa: the first 15 years');
– working with their direct surroundings, the space and the people (for ruangrupa this space is mainly the city of Jakarta, and often also the world at large);
– etc.

3.2.1.3 Why these specific examples?

What follows are four examples of two artists and two artists' collectives. I have limited myself here to describing examples related to the concept of also-space. A general discussion of alternative space, also-space and negotiation space will come later, in an insert at the end of this chapter.

These are concrete examples of practices, which provide a hint of what an also-space could be like. I have chosen to describe these four different types of practitioners in order to provide a broader perspective. Talking to different Indonesian artists or art initiatives, I sensed some opposition against the term 'also-space'. I should say that also-space is not a fixed term but a working term. In that sense it's comparable to anarchism, which has no fixed definition either. Anarchy is not something you can do, it is a part of being active, and an anarchist way of doing things depends on the context, situation, etc. Solidarity economy is another such fluid term; Ethan Miller, a practitioner/theorist of community economies, describes solidarity economy as:

> *'[...] an open process, an invitation. The concept does not arise from a single political tradition or body of ideas. Its very nature and definition are in continual development, discussed and debated among its advocates. Seeking to "make the road by walking" rather than to push a closed or finalized ideology, solidarity economy is a "movement of movements" continually seeking connections and possibilities while holding*

5 The Gezi Park protests were a wave of demonstrations and civil unrest in 2013 in Turkey, following a violent crackdown against a peaceful sit-in protesting against an urban redevelopment plan for Istanbul's Gezi Park. The demonstrations soon escalated into wider protests against the authoritarian Turkish government.

6 Stedelijk Museum, 'SMBA: Made in Commons', 2013-2014. Accessed online Jan. 1, 2015. *http://stedelijk.nl/en/exhibitions/sm*

on to the transformative commitment of shared values.' [7]

One could also argue that fluid structures are by definition tricky. Activists and artists may end up weakening themselves through such fluid structures. This is exactly how neoliberal systems seduce us, by framing every measure as a next step in a fluid structure serving individual freedom. Artists and activists must always find a balance between taking a stance and being pragmatic. Let us not be naïve; there is no other way out, or as Roel in 't Veld says,[8] all is already lost. To be able to act strategically, artists need first to connect to their everyday life of being active, and to build up from there. As ruangrupa did: just start from friendship and see where that leads to, find out what friendship is really capable of. From there, artists and activists can find out what actual power is, and how they can find their role in this power.

Having said that, let us now examine some aspects of these four practices.

My descriptions of the collectives Lifepatch and Jatiwangi Art Factory are first-hand observations. My text about the artist Moelyono is based on a text by the researcher Nuraini Juliastuti as well as notes from a discussion organised by KUNCI, Cultural Studies Centre in Yogyakarta in the context of the project 'Made in Commons', 2014. The text about the artist Wok the Rock (Woto Wibowo) is based on a text sent to me personally by Nuraini Juliastuti and a text published in the catalogue of the 2013 Jakarta Biennale.

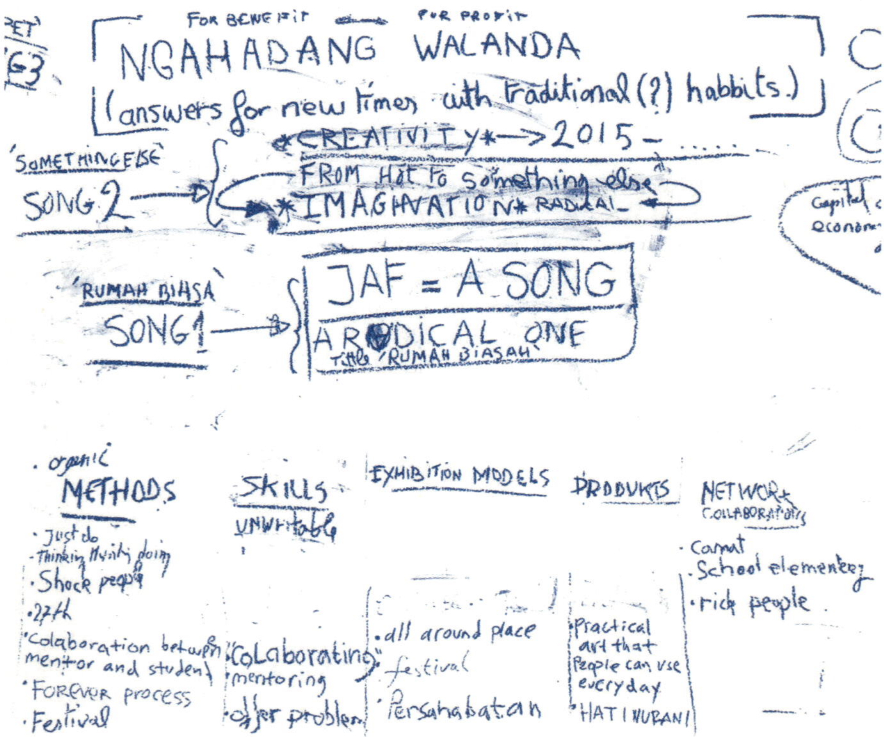

7 Ethan Miller, 'Solidarity Economy Key Issues', in: E. Kawano, T. Masterson and J. Teller-Ellsberg (eds.), *Solidarity Economy I: Building Alternatives for People and Planet.* Amherst, MA: Center for Popular Economics. 2010.

8 Roel in 't Veld gave a talk at a conference organised by Freehouse ('Freehouse: Radicalizing the Local') in Rotterdam, Jan. 22-23, 2014.

3.3 Practitioners

3.3.1 Lifepatch

http://lifepatch.org

Citizen initiative in art, science and technology

Members (2015): Agus Tri Budiarto, Nur Akbar Arofatullah, Budi Prakosa, Andreas Siagian, Agung Geger, Arifin Wicaksono, Adhari Donora, Ferial Afiff, Wawies Wisnu Wisdantio.

> *'Lifepatch is a citizen initiative that works in creative and effective applications in the fields of art, science and technology. In its activities, Lifepatch's practices focus on the arts and educations in science and technology that are practical and useful for citizens around them. This is done through with the development of creative and innovative practices in technology such as biological technology, environmental technology and digital technology. In practice, Lifepatch enriches the culture emphasizes on the spirit of DIY and DIWO by inviting designated public to be involved, to examine, explore, develop and maximize the function of technology in both the theoretical and practical use to society and culture itself.'*
>
> *Grace Samboh, in an a text sent to me by e-mail on Lifepatch. In this e-mail she also said: 'I wrote an intro on Lifepatch but haven't had the chance to expand or update them to an essay', July 2014.*

PLATFORM: ANY PLACE IS A STAGE	COLLABORATORS AND PRODUCERS	CONCERNS	METHODS	ART
There is not really a public or audience. Lifepatch conducts projects and shares knowledge through workshops and collaborations. People are connected by participating or attending public moments (exhibitions, events, etc.) In one project in a museum, Lifepatch gave a child the opportunity to show her works. Providing this child (and indirectly also her family) with a stage, rather than emphasising their own role in 'curating' these works On other occasions they will present results of earlier activities in a more formal and archival (artefact) format	Socio-cultural communities Friends Villagers Teachers Children Students City dwellers Makers community International network of new media Etc.	Education Biology Understanding science (new and traditional) Trust in ability of citizens Sharing of knowledge Etc.	All members bring in their own field of interest Led by curiosity, friendship and citizenship Anything can happen Applied thinking such as: linking street murals to a digital map, connecting street artists with cycling community Etc.	Art is not that important yet. Lifepatch member Andreas Siagian: *'Just use a set of technical skills and work together, search or use collaborations to develop your own language [...] in a mindset of communing. Look for interaction, develop activities within the context you really relate to. Base these activities on personal relations.'*

Lifepatch is a collective of nine people from different backgrounds and different fields of interest. Some have a technical background in science, others are part of the cycling community of Yogyakarta. One is a bookkeeper, the other is an architect interested in urban development. One person is simply there, another is attracted to photography, etc.

Lifepatch was founded relatively recently, in 2012. Since then Lifepatch has been finding its way as an open-structured collective. It's nice to see how they, in a seemingly natural way, just breathe the air where they are and work with that substance. A motto of being active could be:

> *'You don't know the result, you are part of the result, it's about organising activities that are an important way of making art. It's about passing ideas on to each other, sharing resources and research. Some can use your resources for experiments, some to discover new methods, sometimes to bring different people together working on a same topic from different angles [...]'*
>
> *Andreas Siagian, in a conversation with me, August 2014.*

Lifepatch's approach could be described as follows: Lifepatch projects are initiated through contacts with friends, neighbours and others. Lifepatch develops ideas based on available knowledge. If there is no specific knowledge available, Lifepatch postpones the project in order to develop more knowledge and subsequently get a better grip on the content of the project in which they have been invited to participate. They are not interested in responding to an invitation if they don't yet have a relationship with the people who invited them.

> *'The main focus of Lifepatch is on sharing knowledge with the people. Until now, there were no formal education options for learning about new media – there is no school for that. At Lifepatch, we question global technologies and science – the trends. We realised that Indonesia lost many traditional sciences during colonisation. We try to bring this specific issue of traditional science into our practices because we think it is very important and very interesting.'*
>
> *Andreas Siagian, in an interview with Rebecca Conroy, Inside Indonesia 118: Oct.-Dec. 2014 (http://insideindonesia.org/between-science-art-and-social-design-there-is-community).*

Though Lifepatch is often described as a 'new media' initiative or collective, for many of its members it is much more than that. Andreas Siagian states that Lifepatch is first and foremost a citizens' initiative. Through Lifepatch, members develop their own interests and empower individuals and communities through their own prior specific knowledge.

3.3.2 JAF, Jatiwangi Art Factory

https://jatiwangiartfactory.wordpress.com

Members (2014): Ismal Muntaha, Arief Yudi Rahman, Ginggi Syarif Hasyim, Deni Aryanto, Ahmad Tian Fulthan, Loranita Theo, Tedi En, Syarif Hidayat (Peyet), Yopie Nugraha, Arie Syarifuddin (Alghorie).

> *'Mimpinya; seni bisa masuk ke dalam anatomi masyarakat paling dalam. Menjadi hubungan antar manusia, menjadi pengingat antar tetangga, menjadi itikad baik'.*
>
> *('The dream was; art can fill in the deepest anatomy of society. Become a human relationship, a reminder between neighbours, a goodwill.')*
>
> *Jatiwangi Art Factory, 2013, a statement on their website.*

Jatiwangi Art Factory (JAF) is an initiative by artists and the head of the village in Jatisura, Indonesia. The village, which is one of 16 villages composing the Jatiwangi district, currently finds itself in a period of transition. Until recently it was the main centre of production of roof tiles in Indonesia. Now Jatiwangi has to find new ways of generating income and thus value. One of the answers is to professionalise the industry. The district will also be transformed by the new Kertajati Airport due to open in 2017 and the arrival of new factories producing consumer goods in the textile industry. Land is cheap, unemployment is high and the area will be within close distance of Jakarta and Bandung once the highway has been built. Since 2005, Jatiwangi Art Factory plays an important role in finding answers to the challenges facing the old social structure of the former roof tile capital. In a second period, since 2010, JAF has been attempting to play a subtle role in shaping the changing social structure of the village. This change was mostly the result of a shift from family-based entrepreneurship to corporate entrepreneurship which is taking over the region (including precarious jobs, shopping malls, investment climate, waste production, etc.).

In 2005, Arief Yudi, originally from Jatisura, began using his parents' house and former roof tile factory as a place to inspire and generate new insights regarding the situation in the Jatiwangi district. Together with his wife Loranita Theo and his brother Ginggi Syarif Hasyim, who became head of the village of Jatisura, they set up a testing ground for artists, students, citizens and other interested people. JAF provides a context for formulating questions and facilitating meaningful encounters, providing insight in the context of Jatiwangi and preparing the ground for possible projects and collaborations with anyone joining them at Jatisura.

In order for this to take place, there is a need for generosity, hospitality, production tools, etc. I like to say that JAF's main interest is to create 'carpets' or 'airstrips' as a curatorial programme. 'Airstrips' because Jatisura is currently not easy to reach: from Jakarta the trip takes three hours by train, followed by more than one hour by car on a very busy road. This is why JAF often refers to itself as an airstrip ('Landasan' in Indonesian). People land and take off again and therefore it is important to be prepared to provide these transitory visitors with basic conditions. And 'carpets' because of the way Indonesian communities tend to receive their guests for a gathering: they spread out a carpet, people gather on it and are served food and drinks and are able to discuss whatever business they came for. It is no surprise that JAF involves not only the neighbours but also a local school, shop owners, and the 'Camat' (the head of the district and the heads of the villages) in their programming, since a connection to one's roots is seen as a valuable and productive resource by many Indonesian art collectives.

PLATFORM: ANY PLACE IS A STAGE	COLLABORATORS AND PRODUCERS	CONCERNS	METHODS	ART
Private houses	Local government	Education	Artist in residence	Encouraging 'cari sendiri' (finding your own way)
Broadcasting video and radio	Informal art network	Organic food	Project residencies in villagers' houses	Visual representation of possibilities for acting and producing
Central meeting hall	Villagers	Trust in ability of citizens	Providing space to meet and reside	Understanding and getting a grip on today's world
Public spaces	Teachers	Sharing of knowledge	Anything can happen	Daring to be radical
Community spaces	Communities	Value production	Adapting social structures (or working 'within')	Research and testing focused on later production and application
School buildings	Students	Everyday life	Networking within the structure of the village	Life as an art form?
Etc.	Etc.		The central hub of JAF is the house consisting of a working hall, bedrooms and a kitchen	

Whether or not JAF and their guests produce 'art' doesn't really matter. It's more important to formulate questions, to generate new insights and bring existing insights to the surface, and to explore further from that point. JAF has done this for example with the Future Festival in 2013, in which JAF collaborated with the villagers in formulating their wishes for the year 2023. Another example is the Family Festival: ten families from outside the Jatiwangi district were invited to stay in the villages for two weeks and were asked to help develop a programme for ten families in Jatiwangi.

Also here, it doesn't matter whether or not what is being produced is 'art'. If producing artworks is only about self-confirmation and applying the same methods as the neoliberal production methods which critical artists are opposed to, then it might be better for critical artists to try something else. What is the value of imagination for an artist? What is it a gLEAP[9] artist is (visually) representing? In which respects is an artist radical? Practices such as those we see at JAF, where it doesn't matter whether something is considered 'art' or not, challenge the very ontological status of art and confront artists with the question of what is it exactly they are producing.

Arief Yudi asks the artists involved in the Village Festival: who is more inventive, who has more authority, the villager or the artist? Arief likes to leave the function of JAF open; he likes to play the role of the one who doesn't know. He wishes to provide a space for young people in which they can be confronted with reality and generate non-capitalist visions together with villagers, thus creating a new force that will hopefully take over Jatiwangi in the near future.

3.3.3 Moelyono

'Artists cannot remain neutral and only treat people as an aesthetic object to produce their work. Artists must provide a way to awaken public awareness. Moelyono named the art activity he conducts with communities as "awakening media".'

2013 Jakarta Biennale catalogue

'Moelyono is an Indonesian artist born in 1957. In some communities in which he has collaborated, he is known as "the drawing man". Since the 1980s Moelyono went steadfastly from village to village, holding art workshops for the villagers and conducting many social, economic and political empowerment activities with them. In 2001 he left for Pune, India, where he learnt from the Early Childhood Care Development program the notions of ahimsa (non-violence and respect for all life) and swadeshi (self-sufficiency). This experience

PLATFORM: ANY PLACE IS A STAGE	COLLABORATORS AND PRODUCERS	CONCERNS	METHODS	ART
Community spaces Art galleries Public spaces School buildings Etc.	Local government Villagers Teachers Communities Students NGOs Etc.	Education Trust in ability of citizens, empowering Sharing of knowledge Visual representation of hidden community structures and concerns	Using the infrastructure of NGOs to reach audiences Drawing workshops Adapting social structures (or working 'within') Networking within the structure of the village	Encouraging 'cari sendiri' (finding your own way) Visual representation of possibilities for acting and producing Showing 'artefacts' of workshops in gallery spaces

9 See section 3.6.1 for a definition of gLEAP.

encouraged Moelyono to practice "holistic education", which is centred on the idea that everything is based on what we already have available; hence a community rich in local culture can initiate its own education system. It can develop its own inherent potentials as teaching modules that can be broken down into different subject areas. Moelyono said to the people of the village of Anyelma: "We don't need to invite teachers from outside the village because we have a wealth of local potential. Those who can sing can be teachers, those who can make a noken can be teachers as well." At this time, Moelyono produced an object that embodied the notion of holistic education. It was a simple bag from unbleached cotton cloth containing a set of educational games and tools made by the family. This "portable school" could be hung from the house walls, taken to the fields or brought into neighbours' houses. Education in this form is based on self-support and a spirit of do-it-yourself, so that every community can set up a school on its own. A community that masters local wisdom becomes its own educational agent. The above outline of Moelyono's practice establishes his methodology and use of art as a means to promote new ways of thinking in society. The effects of his practice still need to be examined.'

Nuraini Juliastuti, 'Moelyono and the Endurance of Arts for Society', in: Afterall, no. 13, Spring/Summer 2006.

After his trip to India, Moelyono came back with a number of new terminologies and insights with which to reframe his artistic practice. Transformation, dialogue and participation became the words he would use to describe his material and practice, rather than paint, ink, expression, etc. In this way Moelyono was able to link his work to activism and to move from 'art for art's sake' towards 'art for the sake of what I can achieve with it'. With his work he stimulates the (personal) production of all participants and documents the ways in which society develops (receiving feedback and activating people). He calls his work 'seni rupa kerja', which roughly translates as 'visual art at work, useful art, stimulating art, etc.'; the translation is difficult as the meaning of the term is somewhat open-ended. Moelyono is known as 'the drawing man' or 'pak moel guru nggambar'. With his drawing classes Moelyono searches for the common ground within a community; getting to know the hidden layers of issues around land ownership, exploring drawing as a way of addressing social issues. He also creates a platform for encouraging people to act, for stimulating physical and mental motor sensitivity. In the beginning Moelyono worked in his own neighbouring community. Afterwards, he travelled to different parts of Indonesia, parts that were new to him, working with various local communities through drawing. He also started working together with NGOs, which was, besides a financial necessity, more importantly a strategic choice: this made it possible for Moelyono to reach more people with his educational method.

While discussing Moelyono's way of working, two important questions arise. First of all, what is commitment? When can or does an artist distance himself from the community he is working with? Or should the artist maintain a relationship with that community? In Moelyono's work it is important that the community can appropriate in their own way the method he has devised, and in order to make this possible he invests a lot of time and dedication in the places where he works. His works are not projects to be produced; rather, projects develop through dialogue and informal contacts.

The second question is related to art production: how can we develop a social value system for Moelyono's practice, as opposed to the value of an artist's work in gallery? Is it an artwork you can look at, or a moment to be experienced and dealt with? It really is a nonsensical question. If a certain type of art is about encouraging (individual) change, how can we put a value on that? If you work so closely with a community and with their children, how can you measure the impact of that work on a social level, or its potential in the near future? Should we use the type of measurements used by public institutes or NGOs, or do we have to formulate a new concept of evaluation and appreciation?

3.3.4 Wok the Rock

'Woto Wibowo, or Wok the Rock, his more popular public name, is a musician and a visual artist based in Yogyakarta. As an artist, his works are based on his histories of friendships. It is the kind of friendship, which borders on the platform of partnership. Collaborators in a partnership can be friends. While building on a state of shared emotions and trust, in the case of Wok, friendship is also continuously seen as an association of labour from which a partnership can be constructed. [...] The idea of "people as infrastructure" proposed by (AbdouMaliq) Simone, derives from the extension of the idea of "infrastructure" to "people's activities". Drawing on Henri Lefebvre's "representations of space" which describes the close interrelation between places, people, actions, and things, Simone's "people as infrastructure" defines adeptness at generating "maximal outcomes" from tentative and precarious process of remaking the city and urban environment, which shapes how one lives, makes things, and collaborates with one another.'

Nuraini Juliastuti, 'Wok the Rock & Co: Making Sense of Friendship in Yogyakarta's Art Scene', unpublished, 2015. This text was sent to me personally by Nuraini Juliastuti by e-mail, and is part of her preparation for a research on Wok The Rock, which was expected to be finished around 2015.

The above quotation tells us that the work of Woto Wibowo / Wok the Rock (also known as WoWo) should not be understood as community art, but rather finds its form through a supportive structure of friendship and togetherness. The work of WoWo can be seen as a community in itself. Wok the Rock once described himself as follows:

'I have no specific style or theme in making an artwork. But I'm always interested to represent the symptoms of social-cultural changes in the place I live. In present days I was inspired by free-culture movement, which is promoting a share culture in exchange of information, knowledge, intellectual works. This concept has influenced the way I worked. By this direction then I produced some appropriation art and get engaged with digital/internet technology. Alongside doing individual works, I'm interested doing a collaborative and interactive art project. Beside visual art, I am also interested in music. I was involved in underground music scene in Yogyakarta. By 2007 I'm running Yes No Wave Music, a net label (internet records label) releasing music album in MP3 format for free download.' [10]

For his contribution to the 2013 Jakarta Biennale, Wok the Rock founded TrashSquad, a punk cleaning crew. He knew from experience that punk-culture youth tend to hang out at places like the evening supermarkets you can find all around Jakarta. Punks are often seen as 'dirty

PLATFORM: ANY PLACE IS A STAGE	COLLABORATORS AND PRODUCERS	CONCERNS	METHODS	ART
Concerts Art galleries Public spaces Website Social media	Friends Artists (Punk) communities Music scene Etc.	Free culture Building communities Useful art?	Using the structure of friendship Social media analog/digital Using network of artists	Sculpture of communities Manager Anarchist / punk attitude Life as an art form?

[10] See *http://rhizome.org/profile/woktherock1/*

troublemakers', but this TrashSquad actually cleans the mess left behind by 'normal people' near the supermarket, while singing marches and patriotic songs.[11]

In WoWo's work and network there is a danger of an internalised discourse: being a member of the Yogyakarta-based photography collective MES 56, running the punk music label Yes Wave No Wave, residing most of the time at the Cultural Studies Centre KUNCI, and otherwise living and working in Yogyakarta, a city with many artists and art communities, it would be easy for him to get stuck in a self-confirming alternative scene.

However, with his project TrashSquad for the 2013 Jakarta Biennale, WoWo shows that it is possible to operate within the public space, that his stage is a stage which is already there. He was asked by the curators to represent (or re-enact) this work in one of the Biennale venues. I discussed with him this logical/illogical request: why would you present this activity in an exhibition space when the work has in fact already been presented, and an archival representation is not that important (yet)?

It was a challenge made up by the curators to provide WoWo with an opportunity to show the work to an art audience, to provide an insight to people who hadn't witnessed the work in action. However, I wonder whether this is really necessary and worth the energy of re-enacting the work in the context of an art exhibition. This request of the curators not only challenged WoWo, it also challenged the curators themselves. Was their request really suitable to WoWo's work? Of course, such a request should in fact be understood as part of an ongoing dialogue on how to deal with this kind of work in the first place. Though on one hand they did compel him to present his work in an unnatural location, on the other hand this can also be seen as a thought experiment by the curators. For this reason Wok The Rock himself tried his best, but didn't really feel comfortable in the context of the art venue.

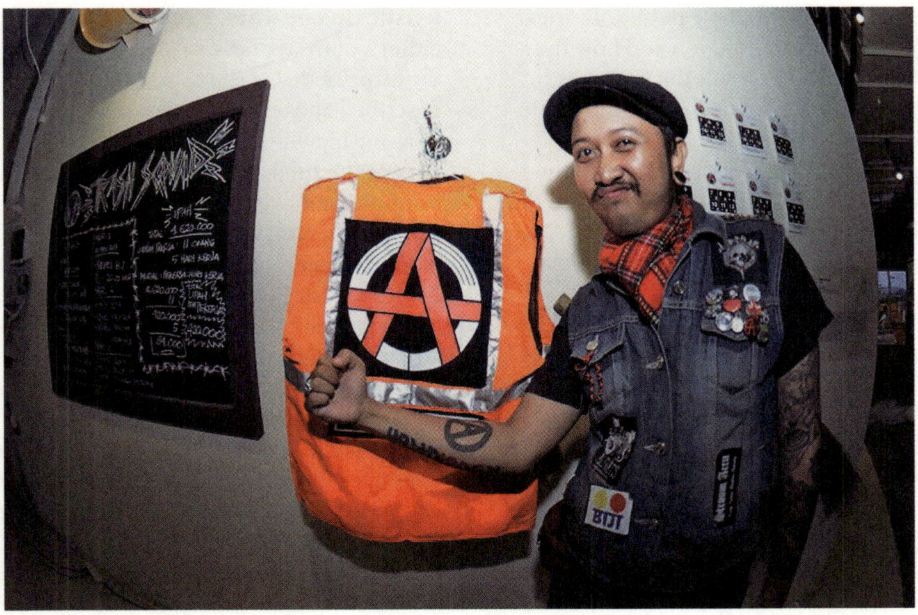

[11] As described in the 2013 Jakarta Biennale catalogue.

3.4 Extracting characteristics for an also-space?

– Stage: In the tables in the preceding pages, I have replaced the word 'exhibition' with the word 'stage' in order to shift the focus toward the public to whom the activities are being addressed. Activities and public moments usually happen at a specific time and place. This should prompt us to think about the limitations of what we can show at (traditional) exhibition spaces and what we can expect from these spaces. When the examples we have considered above are presented in more traditional exhibition spaces, we see that the exhibition often consists of archival 'artefacts' of previous activities. A stage, however, can be set up anywhere, anytime. An exhibition or a stage is a 'public moment' and the 'white cube' habitat of fine art usually isn't the most suitable place for communicating (with the intended audience). People visiting such art spaces are only a small percentage of the intended audience. On the other hand I do understand that a museum, a gallery, an institution can provide continuity, accessibility, a neutral place or a safe haven, and so the need for such places is quite understandable (as for example public libraries are); but how they function and how they are equipped doesn't suit the practices described above, nor the (supposed) ambition of much critical art.

– Audience: There is a certain contextual logic in who exactly is considered to be the audience, who is involved in projects. The audience is often the people who are the direct actors in the matter at hand. The work is human so to speak, it breathes. It's not *about* issues or people, it's *with* people and it makes connections between issues that are of interest to people. However, in the case of a show at a gallery or an art institution, the audience is little more than a passive spectator. The audience remains at a safe distance from interesting topics, whether or not the works are (so-called) interactive.

– Influence in the making process: There is a dialogue during the making process, the work is influenced by third parties. The activity or the work is often done collectively or influenced by people passing by, a possible audience. An artist requires a certain concentration or contributes a specific quality, but the work is often at its best when it is related to other activities, like-minded energies in different layers of society or disciplines. (I would go so far as to call this 'transdisciplinary' in a very real sense, as well as citizenship-related).

– The artist's own production: Artists should worry less about their status as an artist, and instead learn to inhabit different roles. The artist can if necessary be active 'merely' as a facilitator, assistant, builder, collaborator, etc. Sometimes artists need to express their own thinking as an individual artwork, sometimes they are only a spectator, etc.

– Taking initiative: Often an artist or a group of artists clearly takes the lead, the initiative. The artist can see possibilities, or can call to action. This is a specific quality and an intelligence of artists. This leadership role is to a great extent confirmed by the role the artist plays in generating empowerment, confidence, support and encouragement of people to believe in their potential.

If I could summarise all of these characteristics in one word, I guess it would be either 'connectedness' or 'embedded'. It is no surprise that the artists and initiatives described above mostly exist in a close relationship with the collaborative partners or the subjects they are working with or upon (and using a specific medium of general interest such as music, photography/video, science, etc.). They all emerged and developed (or literally grew up) with some of the typical Indonesian characteristics of an understanding of living together.[12] The subjects of their work are the environments which the artists themselves are a part of.

One could say that the artists and initiatives operate on both a literal and an abstract level. They begin by working from a concrete subject or situation, and in the best case the work refers to its specific situation or context, as well as to a more abstract level of understanding mechanisms of citizenship, etc.

12 See chapter 2, section 2.2.3.2, 'Indonesian customs that have shaped ruangrupa'.

3.5 To outline also-space

In the context of ruangrupa and the other examples of Indonesian artists and collectives through which I am illustrating this notion of also-space, what I mean to say by the diagram on these pages is that as artists develop a clearer and more practical understanding of the meaning of citizenship, or of that which ruangrupa calls 'the various transactions', they become more accomplished in applying their artistic practice within the context of this citizenship. Ruangrupa has been increasingly using the word 'transactions' to describe the formal and informal activities which residents engage in with each other; by observing and identifying the wide variety of informal relationships, these activities can be made visible, or a project based on these activities can be initiated.

The activities and persons being studied can for example be providers of information, participants, an audience; or simply (momentary) neighbours, fellow citizens, etc. Such practices do not necessarily yield solutions immediately applicable in society, but rather serve to collectively define the existing (also-) narratives, as absurd and impractical as these sometimes may seem. In a focused setting, such as that attempted by HomeShop,[13] this contributes to building an also-world, an also-possible arrangement or design of the social and political environment.

We can see that:

– An also-space, as we have already noted, is essentially the result of an understanding that we are all active parts of a community/society. An important task for artists is to question their own ideas, and to test these ideas against the various valid visions of how a society could be designed.

– It requires a great deal of energy to work and think this way, since all of the structures we are used to working in are focused on promoting competition and protecting individual interests. However this approach also gives a great deal of energy which would otherwise be wasted on competition and opposition; in this view of things, conflicts are seen instead as dialogues, or at least provide some space for different views and different ways of doing things. The development of knowledge is seen as an ongoing process, and consequently a (temporary) lack of knowledge or understanding is accepted as an integral part of this process.

– An also-space can be based on individual fields of interest or motivations, as well as on the wishes of a community.

– An also-space is always open to finding new partners and meeting kindred spirits in various communities. These kindred spirits are not necessarily to be found in your own circle of friends and colleagues. Sometimes a family doctor will happen to be closer to your mentality and approach than a colleague artist with whom you share a studio.

– An also-space is a testing ground in which to develop an artistic practice together *with* others, rather than *for* others or *for* an audience. By applying skills, insights and the curiosity of others and yourself. By being in a state of dialogue with the environment (literally and figuratively), stimulated by the insights or projects of other people, etc.

– Building networks which allow us to strengthen our position, which in turn allows us to help develop each other's vocabulary and provide each other with input.

– Ultimately it's all about how socio-political spaces can be designed, how we reflect upon such processes, how we bring to light different ways of doing things, how we draw attention to the visible and the invisible.

To summarise: the themes or topics of an also-space, loosely related to the notion of citizenship, are always connected to that which is already present. In contrast, artists and art institutes in countries such as the Netherlands and Belgium tend to work on projects with broader or more abstract themes, and to remain at a certain distance from their subjects. On a conceptual level the subjects themselves may be interesting, but they fail to connect to what is already happening or what is in development. Thus we tend to exclude ourselves from the themes

13 See publications by HomeShop: *Wear*, 2009, *Wear 2*, 2011 and *Appendix*, 2012.

we would like to work with, or we use a language that is not related to the subjects we are talking about. I would say that artists and institutes thus tend to live too much in a not-so-relevant 'utopia'.

3.6 Moving on

3.6.1 gLEAP

I became closely involved with ruangrupa shortly after it was founded in 2000. Ruangrupa has always been a 'sparring partner' which has helped me to understand and improve my own practice as an artist and as a citizen. My personal doubts about the art world, and at the same time my stubborn persistence in continuing to operate within this world, were to some degree confirmed by what I encountered there. Ruangrupa also served as an important source of inspiration in defining my attempt at formulating a '(g)Locally Embedded Art Practice' (gLEAP), an art practice that attempts to reconfigure the relation between the artists' everyday life/activity and their artistic production.

As I have said before, it is highly problematic when artists/citizens (working towards social change) define their activities as 'alternative'. As the Brazilian philosopher Rodrigo Nunes, a member of the editorial collective of the news blog 'Turbulence', explains in his book 'Organisation of the Organisationless':

> *'The non-debate between the for and against camps, and the distorted picture of what we do that results from it, has become a hindrance to posing questions concerning the exercise of power, political organisation, and how to effect social change, and to finding the ways in which these can be posed in a new situation. We are certainly not lacking in urgent reasons to do so'.* [14]

We are aware that we are being indoctrinated by thinking in oppositions; consider for example political campaigns, the patent industry, the media industry, ethnic differentiation, international sports competitions such as the Olympics, etc. It may be more productive to consider instead what the 'opposing party' thinks and does as 'also-ways' of designing our environment. Critical citizens are not in opposition to the world; rather, they are part of the world, just like everybody else. I am not talking here about 'community art' or 'participatory art'; rather, I am searching for specific places and forms of 'publicness', and discovering what I see as contextually logical ways of collaborating and sharing knowledge, in order to arrive at another way of developing an artistic practice, which I am still in the process of defining more clearly; for the time being I have called it gLEAP.

Artists who practice gLEAP do not act alone. They are part of a network of people working on creating a possible world, an also-world that exists alongside the centralised world that many people do not really like but which most of us still unwillingly support. We vote, we sell or buy artworks, we take city trips, we depend upon the banks, we like gadgets and apps, we sometimes buy into retirement plans, etc. There is an acute awareness of the contradiction between on one hand our thinking, and on the other hand our way of living and acting; however, the following step, bringing the two together, often feels obscured or remains plainly absent. We observe that the content and concept of artworks are often out of sync with the everyday activities and production of artists (their ways of living, socialising, buying things, but also their ways of producing artworks, etc.) I would like to think a step further. One definition of gLEAP would be to say that artists build together with and within communities. When artists become a substantial part of the subject of their work, then they also share a long-term commitment to the projects they are involved in.

By studying a model of also-space, artists could gain a clearer understanding of their own practice. This in turn could help solve the discrepancy between their thoughts/wishes and what they actually do. What I believe is really needed is an opening up of the notion of 'autonomous practices' (the fine arts), which seems to be embedded in the DNA of most Western European artists. There is nothing particularly interesting or challenging about artists claiming their individual autonomy in this day and age; indeed,

14 Rodrigo Nunes, *Organisation of the Organisationless: Collective Action After Networks*, Mute/PML Books, 2014, p. 12.

it seems a rather quaint and outdated romanticist position. It may be more interesting to speculate instead about a collective autonomy. According to the cultural theorist, writer, critic and activist Brian Holmes,

> *'Autonomy means giving yourself your own law. But men and women are social beings; we only exist as "ourselves" through the language of the other, through the sensations of the other; and what is more, this shared language, these transiting sensations, are bound up in the uncertainty of memory and forgetting, the incompleteness of perception, the wilfulness of imagination. Thus the attempt to give oneself one's own law becomes a collective adventure, as well as a cultural and artistic one.'* [15]

This is the space which is understood and inhabited by most of the artists and collectives I have described here. They do not merely address themselves to an art scene, but in fact employ a variety of perspectives in their discourse and their actions. This way they avoid the dilemma that Jennifer Smailes pointed out when she criticised Claire Bishop for asking:

> *'[...] for an art that "address[es] this contradictory pull between autonomy and social intervention". As valid as this argument is, its blind spot is that it poses the contemplation of art – with all its potential of emancipation and insight – above other possibly emancipating forms of cultural experience, ignoring that this kind of reception is relevant (and relevant it is) only to a narrow and defined group of people. She thus makes the same mistake of underestimating her own position within the institution of art.'* [16]

What Smailes describes here must certainly be the biggest trap (and reality) of any potentially interesting art programme or project. But perhaps an even more worrisome reality is that hardly any Dutch and Belgian art institutes (or artists) are equipped to avoid this trap. Most of them are not even aware of it yet, and therefore haven't really rethought the nature of their working and presentation spaces.

It cannot be overemphasised that formulating an also-space by definition generates a space for individuals in which to connect. As pleasant as it can be to stroll around with our own concerns and ideas, sometimes it can be even more interesting and fruitful to connect to other people and share these ideas. Some people/artists may have difficulties in connecting and will do so in a clumsy way, but who cares? There are always valid reasons for connecting to others, however impossible it may seem. A jump into the unknown, with a certain confidence that there are in fact possibilities for connecting our own ideas with those of others.

3.6.2 Art school practice: an institute

In Dutch and Belgian art schools, the main goal of art is usually 'to be autonomous and making authentic works of art in which one expresses one's individuality'.[17] In this text written in English, Hans Abbing, a Dutch artist and art theoretician, use two terms that have a somewhat different meaning in Dutch: 'autonomous' which is a Dutch term for fine art, and 'authentic' which also means 'original'.

The framework provided to students, in the perspective of their future artistic practice (and creative entrepreneurship), is mainly an established vision of how the (alternative) art world is organised. The problem with this framework is that its seemingly independent/autonomous attitude is in fact a myth, since, as I have said before, alternative art is itself a myth.

---

15 During a conference at the Tate Modern, London, October 25, 2003, titled 'Diffusion: Collaborative Practice in Contemporary Art'. Also present were Bureau d'études, Francois Deck, Eve Chiapello, Jochen Gerz, Stephen Wright, John Roberts, Charles Green, and others.

16 Jennifer Smailes. 'Being radical. Gently', in: *Newpaper #2: The Autonomy Project*, Onomatopee 43.1. A project by the Van Abbe Museum, Eindhoven, 2010. (*http://theautonomyproject.ning.com*).

17 Hans Abbing, 'The Autonomous Artist still Rules the World of Culture: A Portrait of the Artist in 2005', in: I. Jansen (ed.), *Artistic Careers and Higher Arts Education in Europe*, Amsterdam, Boekmanstudies, 2004, pp. 55-66.

This framework is related to a capitalist value system that emphasises visibility and financial success. It is framed within a Western perspective on exchange and dialogue, constructed around a copyright-protected production of artworks. The system produces artists who, at the end of the day, tend to distance themselves from the communities in which they are living. Art students are trained:

– to provide 'the public' with other perspectives on reality (often in a naïve way);
– to experiment (formally) with material;
– to increase general awareness of public/social issues.

In addition to this programme, art schools also inevitably function as extensions of the political agendas of the countries they happen to be in. This effectively hinders the possibility of allowing art students to arrive at certain types of understanding, at least as long as the educational system is supposed to have some kind of controlling function, as it does now.

> *'With its call for realism, the currently prevailing neoliberalism attempts to reduce this kaleidoscope of approaches to a single perspective, that of the free market. The push to be more entrepreneurial and to embrace the creative industry is supposed to convince us that only one world matters.'*
>
> *Pascal Gielen, 'Autonomy via Heteronomy', OPEN! Platform for Art, Culture and the Public Domain, October 1, 2013.*

Art institutions such as art schools are trapped in this situation and there's no way out; all they can do is go on running around in a closed circle. It's a tricky situation, as these institutions go on behaving as though they are already 'perfect actors' (see also the quote by Cindy Milstein below). The situation outlined by Pascal Gielen is easy enough to recognise; however another important step is missing. Gielen still talks of a modern hope for autonomy. But the friction or polarisation between on one hand neoliberalism, and on the other hand the concept of autonomy, leads only to false choices and non-existent alternatives. The concept of autonomy does not show the way to a truly autonomous art practice, while neoliberalism leads mainly to inefficient and speculative art-market practices.

I cannot teach my students art. The only thing I can do is ask them to consider their context, to work and talk with people and to try to form an understanding of this context. There is no art, as we know it, that can be taught. There is a profession that can be taught, but the question is: what kind of background does this profession exist in?

Why is teaching art all about understanding context, and why should we bother reconsidering the alternative art space? The anarchist activist Cindy Milstein writes:

> *'We tear each other apart in so many varied ways in our social spaces, along so many lines of hurt already inscribed into our bodies by white supremacy, heteronormativity, patriarchy, ableism, settler colonialism, classism, overdetermined identity politics, and a long lineage of other violences. It's frequently assumed that the tag "social space" (or radical bookstore, collective café, bike co-op, and so on) has already done the work for us, as if we are already those perfect actors in our perfectly alternative places.'* [18]

We understand that we will have to drastically change some of our habits, but simply going to a bike co-op, working together on a project with a community, or participating in a balcony farm project won't be enough to change our behaviour, our mentality. There is another level of commitment required, another level of understanding of being together, other perspectives on designing a world.

3.6.3 On a more personal note

Thanks to ruangrupa and other also-activities in which I have been engaged over the years,[19]

---

18 Cindy Milstein, 'Organising Social Space', in: *Roar Magazine*, June 13, 2014. Online journal. Accessible through *http://roarmag.org*

19 The most important of these were: 'Also-Space', which consisted of two exhibitions in Beijing; two events in De Player in Rotterdam, a platform for performative art which, at the time I was involved with it, worked with and within a neighbourhood;

I understand better now my early intuitive doubts about this alternative art scene; I also understand my own moves which led to a next step that is, in fact, already there. Still, I needed to write this text in order to make it all more explicit. Twenty years after I first came to live in to the Netherlands, my idealistic practice of being in a constructive state of dialogue and exchange can now be reframed.

Life is a mix of relations and relationships, of poetry, power, joy, facts, sorrow, mistreatment, abuse, unforeseen events, etc.

We all are part of this composition in which we act, search, unite, find, fundamentally disagree, share our positions. Why should artists hide in their own established spaces? Why should artists only confirm their own assumptions and work alone, without others taking part in this work? I am not pleading here for an instrumentalisation of art, nor for artists to make only social art or to work collaboratively; not at all. That would imply a limited view of what artists do and can do.

I also know we shouldn't underestimate the audience, and yes, I too like to stroll around in art spaces such as Witte de With in Rotterdam, Wiels in Brussels, Extra City in Antwerp, Kunst-Werke in Berlin, P//////AKT in Amsterdam, etc. I like browsing through art books and reading articles on e-flux and in Afterall. On the other hand I believe it's important to realise that these spaces also serve to confirm a world which we don't necessarily want to be part of. It's still a copyright-protected world, a world for individual profit, a men's world, a scene for insiders, and although it may appear to be a generous world, it is not.

For me, this whole exercise of writing and understanding the practices with which I have found so much common ground, is a belated investigation into the kind of practice I see for myself, as well as how I have worked up to this point. With all my likes and dislikes of being and existing in the art world, it was never very clear to me what it is exactly that moves and inspires me. Through this writing I hope to help myself, my friends and my students to gain a better understanding of how we do art and how we ideally would like to do it.

I should clarify once again that the categories of spaces I have described here (and defined more in detail in the insert at the end of this chapter: alternative space, ethical also-space, DIWO also-space, negotiation space, etc.) should be understood as merely a working example within this particular research; a method for shedding light upon the ways in which artists can become aware of their intentions, and how these intentions are realised, or are not. I hope this text can lead to some discussions and ideas that can be tested in the real world. More generally, this is my goal for my own (teaching) practice in the art school and within my professional network.

I'm not there yet. You can see this by the references included in this publication, which are more often than not still from representatives of a specific cultural background.

There are of course artists and movements outside of my interest in Indonesian art practices which I find interesting and worth mentioning here: for example, the FLOK society, an open source art project; new political movements such as Podemos in Spain; artist-run organisations such as Constant in Brussels; artists such as Guy van Belle and Jef Geys, etc. Also, organisations such as Casco in the Netherlands are inspiring because of their diverse approach to programming and connecting networks. W139 in Amsterdam is also an interesting case, as it is now going back to its roots after having had professional curators run the organisation since about 1997. Although the question now is whether they will be are able to go beyond the 'alternative art only' discourse in which they were grounded in the early 1980s...

I'm not sure if ruangrupa really is something else. The art world, which ruangrupa is certainly a part of, is a corrupted world in which everyone is constantly networking, working hard to be or remain visible and

Casco, a centre for art, design and theory in Utrecht with a public program which I regularly attend; HomeShop, an artists' initiative that existed from 2008 to 2012 in Beijing; RTVP1, a travelling exhibition for one person at a person's house, without opening hours or an art audience, organised by Hans Bossmann.

valuable, always worrying about their reputation. These are things that all of us who are active in the art world have to deal with in one way or another. But how we understand them and bring them in practice, that's where the difference is.

Poetry, fiction, narrative, hacking, documenting, working together are all possible ways of suggesting a road towards something else, or of providing and sharing insights in those places where it already is happening. As I was writing this text, I came to appreciate and even admire people who are involved both theoretically and practically with their own practice from the perspective and level of citizens, in a way that I would call transdisciplinary for want of a better word. This way we can merge different worlds, allowing us to influence both the political world (negotiation space) and the world of grassroots activities (also-space).

I'd like to end with a thought by the American media theoretician Mark Poster. Not only does he reflect upon the digital world as part of our everyday lives, which is a dimension I have not touched upon enough in this research; more importantly, he provides a clear insight into why we have to give up an essential part of ourselves in order to create space in which an also-space can occur. This is part of a debate that has been going on since the 1990s, however it also exemplifies how little has changed:

> *'I want to suggest in this essay, in the spirit of my epigraph from Jean Baudrillard, that Western concepts and political principles such as the rights of man and the citizen, however progressive a role they played in history, may not provide an adequate basis of critique in our current, increasingly global condition. They may not provide, that is, a vehicle for thinking through and mobilizing a planetary democratic movement. This is so for three reasons. First, the simple fact that these principles derive from the West, which is responsible for an imperialist and capitalist form of globalization, detracts from their ability to catalyse truly global movements against domination; the origin of these principles makes one suspicious of them from the start. Second, the situation today calls for democratic principles that include difference with universality, that cover the peoples of the earth but acknowledge situational differences. Enlightenment principles are deficient here because they move to the universal too quickly, forgetting their conditions of possibility in an emergent bourgeoisie of the eighteenth century. In the rush to insist on democracy and humanity, in the intoxication with the idea of democracy, in the irrefutable radicalism of such ideas in the context of the waning of the Old Regime in Europe, the principles of natural right required one to extract oneself from the social in order to proclaim the universal as natural. Third, today the natural no longer exists as an autonomous realm of self-determination. Today science and technology constitute a humanized nature and in so doing bring forth machines. The conditions of globalization are not only capitalism and imperialism; they include the linking of human and machine. New democratizing principles must take into account the cultural construction of the human-machine interface. In short, we may build new political structures outside the nation-state only in collaboration with machines. The new community will not be a replica of the agora, but it will be mediatized.'* [20]

What does this mean for an art practice? How can we make democratic art? One thing we can learn from the examples from Indonesia is that a critical (citizen-related) art practice doesn't necessarily start from critique, or from an individualist independent ('autonomous') position. The Indonesian activist artist doesn't begin with critique, but works from an acceptance of a given starting position. Though an individual's thoughts and intentions are often a leading force in realising things, in the end the goal of these thoughts is always to generate content, to develop interesting ideas, with individual authorship being ultimately irrelevant. The formation of a collective of citizens is not a programme written by individuals. The genius only exists as a collective, even if this slows things down or makes them more complicated.

20 Mark Poster, 'Digital Networks and Citizenship', in: *PMLA*, vol. 117, no. 1, Special Topic: Mobile Citizens, Media States, January 2002, pp. 98-103.

It was never my intention to write this text alone. I wanted to write it collaboratively with members of ruangrupa and members of the former HomeShop collective. Yet I was not successful in clarifying who exactly was this 'we' that would be working collaboratively on this text…

3.7 Conclusion: Is there a 'something else'?

Theoretically, yes. In reality, we can only try.

I hesitate to propose to others how they can or should conduct their profession. Also, I have often been sceptical towards collaborative practices or social art projects. It appeared to me that in the end, everyone tended to stick too much to their own point of view, or the activity remained solely within an art discourse. In my own practice, too, I have been mostly unable to successfully negotiate the pitfalls of the contemporary art world. Also, I am quite sceptical of contemporary 'hypes' such as urban farming, time banks, makers' communities and certain forms of sustainable entrepreneurship.[21]

Nevertheless I am convinced that artists should radically change direction, not only in the way they produce artworks, but also in where to present these works and whom to address them to. What matters is that we should truthfully relate to, and be a part of, the different communities in which we live. We should see ourselves as part of a network that can influence, encourage and provide feedback focused on the creation of an also-possible world.

What I'm really interested in here is a model of the ethical also-space, that focuses on designing an also-possible world from practical/speculative/fictional motives. HomeShop did this for a while. Most of its former members still do. We are going 'from hot to something else' anyway; even if we don't know yet what the 'something else' will look like, we still need to prepare for it. Many of us are already engaged in this, in focused and/or playful ways, using both social and digital channels.

Rather than entrenching themselves within a narrowly defined counter-movement, artists and other 'creative practitioners' should rather seek to be part of a broad movement that organically develops from the strengths and capacities of all its participants.

FROM HOT…		… TO SOMETHING ELSE
Profit-driven, market-driven		Benefit-driven, community-driven
Networking in order to increase one's visibility within the art scene	networking	Networking in order to learn and share knowledge
Individual careers	effort	Working towards common goals
Effort to be seen; energy is focused on being represented, on being present and valuable, on being credited	value visibility reputation	Effort to engage with and relate to the context of everyday production; effort to give and receive
Internal community		Different communities

[21] As depicted in the Dutch TV programme 'Wie zijn de mensen van nu?' (literally: 'Who are the people of now?'), September 2013, produced by Tegenlicht (*http://tegenlicht.vpro.nl*).

Insert to Chapter 3

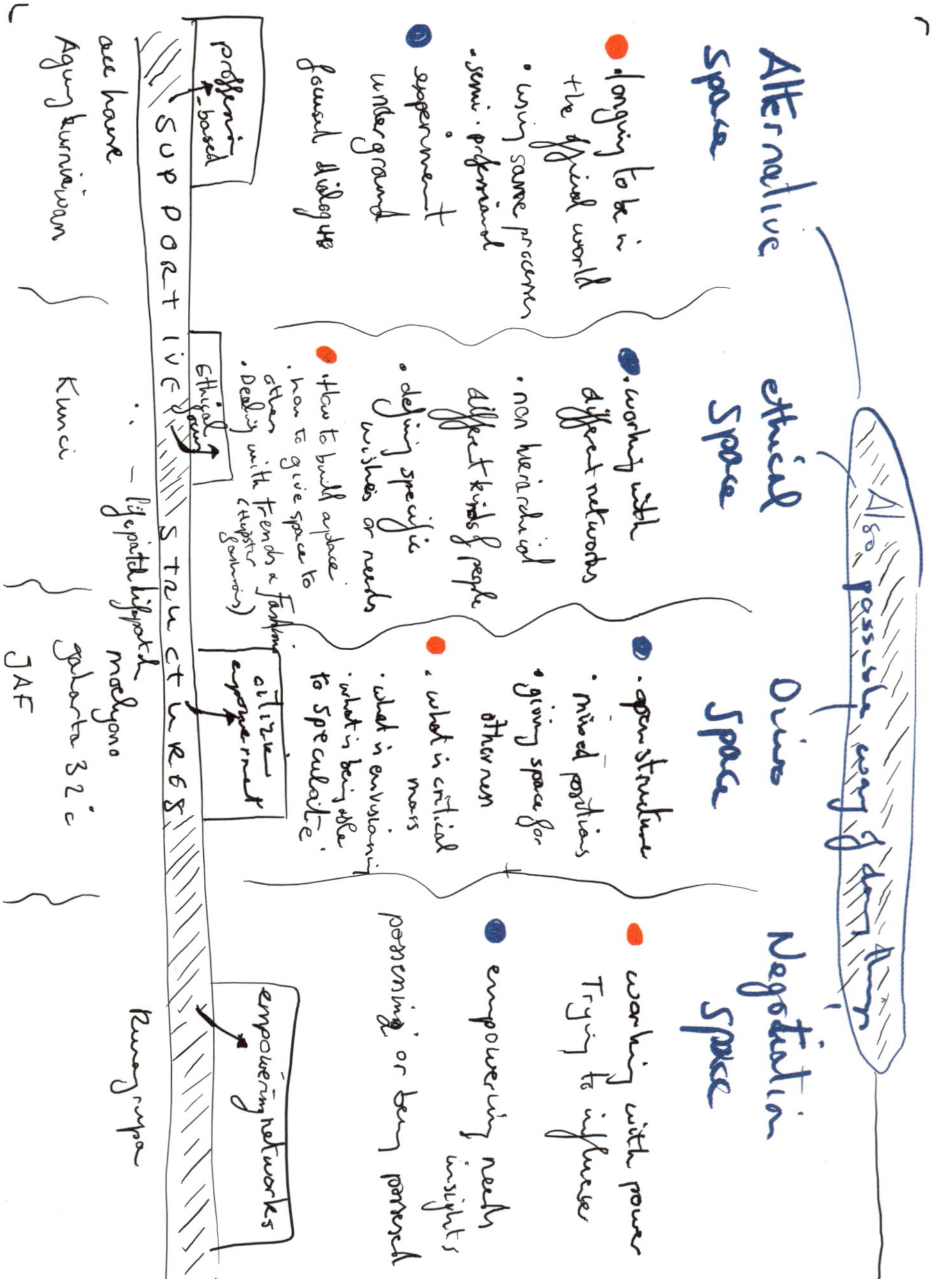

The different types of spaces outlined:

1 Alternative space: of or by a group of friends or like-minded people.

2 Also-space: in combination with everyday activities. I distinguish two types of also-space: the ethical also-space and the DIWO ('do-it-with-others') also-space. The activities of the ethical also-space are guided by a focused field of interest (for example the theory and practice of community building within an urban environment). The DIWO variant is more flexible and open to whatever or whoever happens to be passing by; it is a prime example of a generous space, guided by the understanding that an artist always exists within a heterogeneous world.

3 Negotiation space: in public structures/institutions.

In this insert I will be examining in detail and comparing these three different types of spaces.

1 Alternative space

A space for exchange between artists and others related to art (writers, organisers, family, etc.).
(Semi-professional), part of mainstream society, the institutionalised art world and the capitalist value system.

NOTE	SPACE (PUBLIC PROGRAMME)	CHARACTERISTICS
Alternative or not? *'Can artistic practices still play a critical role in a society where the difference between art and advertizing have become blurred and where artists and cultural workers have become a necessary part of capitalist production? Scrutinizing the 'new spirit of capitalism' Luc Boltanski and Eve Chiapello[1] have shown how the demands for autonomy of the new movements of the 1960's had been harnessed in the development of the post-Fordist networked economy and transformed in new forms of control. The aesthetic strategies of the counterculture: the search for authenticity, the ideal of self-management, the anti-hierarchical exigency, are now used in order to promote the conditions required by the current mode of capitalist regulation, replacing the disciplinary framework characteristic of the Fordist period. Nowadays artistic and cultural production play a central role in the process of capital valorization and, through 'neo-management', artistic critique has become an important element of capitalist productivity.'* Chantal Mouffe, 'Artistic Activism and Agonistic Spaces', in: *Art & Research*, Vol. 1, No. 2, Summer 2007.	The art space as a stage for showing.	Supportive structure for a group, a scene, a closed community. Platform for experimentation amongst peers with the goal of eventually taking part in an official/professional art world. The artist is usually preoccupied with the concerns of her/his own work. Production of original artworks (individual claim of authorship) often within a liberal-democratic mindset. The community 'performs' an alternative lifestyle that is not that far from the mainstream. This is of course nothing new, consider for example the history of punk: *'Punk broke all the rules and declared war on all previously existing musical trends and rules of social behaviour. Rebelling against established musical trends and social mores, punk quickly became a tradition in itself – a movement with highly predictable stylistic elements.'* Henry Tricia, *Break All Rules! Punk Rock and the Making of a Style*, 1989. Question: what is it exactly that makes something 'alternative'?
	either: When it is really necessary to be 'alternative' and somehow isolated from a larger audience: Private locations, going underground. Art for artists (closed circle), friends, family, local art scene, etc. Being alternative within a specific art world, in which one positions oneself simultaneously as insider and outsider (the 'outsider' being a brand consumed by the insider).	
	or: When there is no other solution than to go underground due to: Working with sensitive material (necessary illegal activities). Functioning as a hideout, a think tank (in theory and/or practice) against authoritarian regimes of power (not only political power). When free speech is too dangerous or precarious.	

2 Also-space

2a Also-space as an ethical space (focusing on the commons)

Building a substantial and real alternative together with cultural actors (communities, artists, individuals, neighbours, etc.) alongside dominant centres of (neo-liberal) culture.

NOTE	SPACE (PUBLIC PROGRAMME)	CHARACTERISTICS
One possible approach to an ethical practice: *'My work on free software is motivated by an idealistic goal: spreading freedom and cooperation. I want to encourage free software to spread, replacing proprietary software that forbids cooperation, and thus make our society better.'* Richard Stallman, 'Copyleft: Pragmatic Idealism', GNU Operating System, *http://www.gnu.org/philosophy/pragmatic.html*	Any suitable place can in principle be a stage. 'Public moments' happen during presentations, workshops, talks, exhibitions. They mostly occur at suitable places such as the dinner table, workshop space, community house, art space, etc. (see reinaart vanhoe, 'At the Gate and at the Table', in: *Appendix*, HomeShop, 2012). Organising moments for meeting (in thinking and doing).	Supportive structure for like-minded people or groups. In the cases of HomeShop and Jatiwangi Art Factory, with a focus on the commons. People linked through a commonly felt and shared urgency. Organising and sometimes restoring a collective memory (since collective memory has often been co-opted by media corporations, etc.). A platform for defining ethics of production, a social space. A specific perspective on how to conceive work and/or projects. Multidisciplinary, different 'layers' of society, curious people, etc. Opposing the state of being 'possessed' (of undergoing certain consumerist-oriented forces). An example: 'Feral Trade', an initiative by the artist Kate Rich, is a postal service for organic food. Feral Trade attempts to bypass not only the corporate postal services but also any other middleman. A viable answer, an also-world that exists alongside a certain authority, the authority of the mainstream. Whether or not one's work is meaningful depends on the process of working together and sharing resources. Tactics. A certain kind of autonomy, sovereignty.
	Working with a diverse group of people, individuals, communities, artists, etc. People with different practical goals (some want to make artworks, some want to invent better medications, some want a cleaner neighbourhood, others are looking into issues of privacy, etc.). Keeping one's focus, working and acting in a way that is grounded within a specific social ethos. Building a community with different kinds of people. Working within a community from one's own potentials and focus, not as a counterforce or opposition against existing institutional or capitalist structures. A possibly agonistic space.	

2b **Also-space as a DIWO (do-it-with-others) space**

Working within a mixed group of people, communities. People bring in their connections, their knowledge, their time, their needs, everyday conversations, etc.
The DIWO also-space could also be seen as normal space/altered space/poetic space/etc.

NOTE

'Just use a set of technical skills and work together, search or use collaborations to develop your own language […] and that of others in the area of citizenship.'
Andreas Siagian (Lifepatch) in a conversation with me, Yogyakarta, 2014.

'The more one pole defines itself in opposition to the other, the less it is possible to maintain the middle ground in which questions that could be pertinent to both – how to balance openness and the aptitude for concerted action, how to be capable of strategic decisions while retaining democracy – could appear.'
Rodrigo Nunes, *Organisation of the Organisationless: Collective Action After Networks*, Mute/PML Books, 2014.

SPACE (PUBLIC PROGRAMME)

Any place is a stage: office, campus, highway, institution, kitchen, street, festivity, river, etc.

Personal relationships built up over a longer period of time.

Working within the existing structures of everyday production; artists and others sharing the vulnerability inherent to everyday life.

Working with different kinds of communities and people without judging who they are or what they do.

Working from what is present, from one's latent strengths.

Starting from everyday life, from being there, informal production, co-production.

CHARACTERISTICS

Generosity as supportive structure, encouraging people ('cari sendiri' = finding your own way).

Platform to work from relationships based on friendship as well as a shared notion of citizenship.

Being 'possessed' is not an issue here. We are already possessed anyway, there is always some (political) power above you (for example, being possessed by the mobile phone industry, the pharmaceutical industry).

Outcomes/work are part of a broader production mechanism. Personal preferences become part of a whole, do not overrule the collective.

Being open to interaction. Making one's ego available to collaboration, to developing together, to communal experimentation.

Platform for confronting one's own activities by working together or by involving different groups of people.

Once in a while, defining some mission points: in which direction would we like to be heading?

Is it important that something is seen as 'art'? Can artists simply use their skills (as artists) and implement these in the everyday practice of living together?

What does this mean for a platform, and what does it mean for being recognised as an artist?

3 Negotiation space

Strategically putting the needs and concerns of a group of artists/citizens on the institutional agenda of cultural and political institutions; making these concerns visible to those in power. Proactively demonstrating that one is an authority in specific areas.

NOTE	SPACE (PUBLIC PROGRAMME)	CHARACTERISTICS
'It is ultimately in the city where the politics and economics of privatization, labour and (im)migration are manifested, dividing it into enclaves of mega-wealth and sectors of marginality. This indicates the need to re-engage the invisible forces that shape the territory, reorganize the systems of urban development, and challenge the political and economic frameworks that have produced the crisis in the first place.' From *Radicalizing the Local*, a brochure accompanying a workshop by Teddy Cruz, Miguel Robles-Duran and Jeanne van Heeswijk with students from the Berlage Institute that took place in the Afrikaanderwijk, a working-class neighbourhood in Rotterdam, 2009.	Institutional stage, political arena, facilitating publicity, etc. The artist as negotiator: working directly with power (political, cultural, religious, institutional, etc.). Bringing together, creating a network of socio-cultural actors. Being able to have an overview of different actors, both informal and formal, in the socio-political field. Being able to make connections.	Drawing attention to the preferences, needs and insights of one's own network. Gaining influence by addressing these preferences and needs on an institutional level. Individual concerns play a minor role here (except the concern of profiling oneself in public, of becoming a spokesperson). Either 'possess' or be 'possessed' (in order to make this possible, one must find partners and be able to generate a certain critical mass). Platform for influencing on an institutional and organisational level. The individual energy is harnessed in order to deal with power structures and everything around that. Being a sparring partner, a catalyst. Strategy, infiltrating.

4 (5, 6, etc.) Contingent space

While conducting research we have a tendency to rationalise and formalise our findings, interpretations and definitions. Whatever our original intention may have been, the models we define tend to divide everyone and everything into categories, even if it was just a temporary model made up on the spot to gain insight into a specific dimension (the quote by Mark Poster in section 3.6.3 of the main text of the present chapter is quite illuminating in this respect).

To me the term 'contingent space' means admitting that our models always lack something, for example an insight into the nearby future. For example, as I am busy writing this research, ruangrupa is already working on discovering another possible definition of institutional space.

'Contingent space' thus stands for all the other possible categories I didn't think of, and which would probably have been just as good as the ones which I did happen to formulate, more or less arbitrarily, based on my own experience and perspective.

I leave it to readers to consider for themselves what these kind of spaces might be for them.

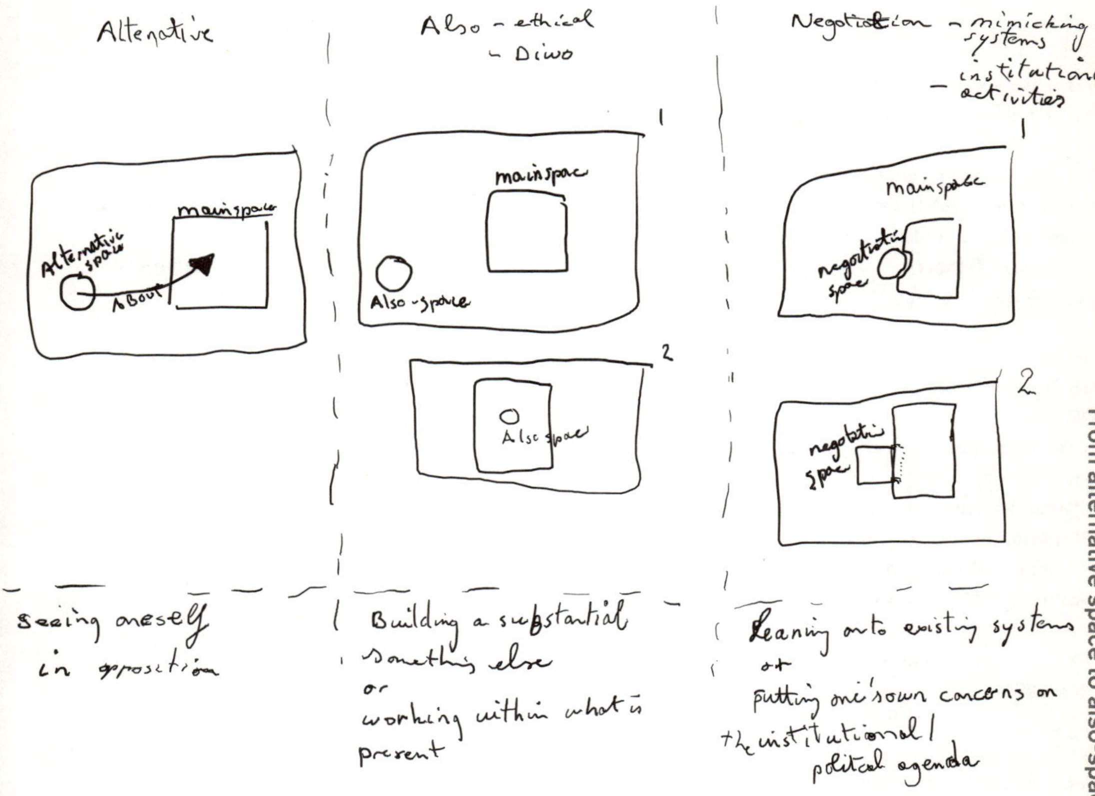
Altenative
mainspace
Alternative space
ABOUT
seeing oneself in opposition
Also – ethical
– Diwo
1
mainspace
Also-space
2
Also space
Building a substantial something else
or
working within what is present
Negotiation – mimicking systems
– institutional activities
1
mainspace
negotiating space
2
negotiation space
Leaning onto existing systems
or
putting one's own concerns on the institutional / political agenda

colophon

Onomatopee 136

Also-Space, **From Hot to Something Else:**
How Indonesian Art Initiatives Have Reinvented Networking

text and illustrations: **reinaart vanhoe**
ISBN: **978-94-91677-59-5**

research guidance: **Florian Cramer**
editing, translation, text design: **Johanna Monk**
readers: **Marielle Verdijk, Sanne Oorthuizen, Hugo Bongers**
graphic design: **Koos Siep**

thanks to:
ruangrupa
KUNCI
CBK Rotterdam
made possible by:
Research Centre Creating 010, Rotterdam University of Applied Sciences
Willem de Kooning Academy, Rotterdam University of Applied Sciences

printed by: **NPN Drukkers**, Breda
edition: 1000

Onomatopee
www.onomatopee.net – info@onomatopee.net
Research Centre Creating 010
www.creating010.com – creating010@hr.nl
reinaart vanhoe and auto
www.vanhoe.org - corporated@gmail.com

All photos by **reinaart vanhoe** or **ruangrupa** except the following:

p. 12: photo by **Jan Kempenaers** (artwork by **Pierre Bismuth**, *'From Hot to Something Else'*)

p. 13 and 18: poster, **Esprit** *'Make Your Wish'* advertisement campaign, 2011, in collaboration with photographer **Yvan Rodic**

p. 22: **Algemeen Dagblad**, *'VN: een mobieltje is makkelijker te vinden dan een wc'*, online newspaper article, March 22, 2013. *http://www.ad.nl/buitenland/vn-een-mobieltje-is-makkelijker-te-vinden-dan-een-wc~a65cf5fa/*

p. 36: **4A Centre for Contemporary Asian Art**, *'Vertical Villages'*, promotional website text, 2013. *http://www.4a.com.au/vertical-villages*

p. 38: anonymous, ruangrupa sticker collection

p. 59: record album cover, *'Radiohead, Ok Computer'*, design by **The White Chocolate Farm**

p. 63: ruangrupa, *'the Kuda'*, cover for mock magazine, 2015

p. 81: photo by **Edo Oktariansyah**